HIP SANTA CRUZ 7

HIP SANTA CRUZ 7

First person accounts of the Hip Culture of Santa Cruz, CA In the 1960's, 1970's, 1980's and Beyond.

1st Edition

Edited by T. Mike Walker

Epigraph Books
Rhinebeck, New York
For information contact:
Epigraph Publishing Service
22 East Market St, Suite 304
Rhinebeck, New York 12572
www.epigraphPS.com

Hip Santa Cruz 7. First person accounts of the Hip Culture of Santa Cruz, California From 1960's - 2024

The Obituary, "Ralph Abraham was always looking for the Big Picture" was first published in Lookout Santa Cruz, Sept. 2024.

Book Layout by Jacob Aman

Book cover & Design by Andrew Cameron Bailey

ISBN: 978-1-966293-07-1
Library of Congress Control Number: 2025904579

Bulk purchase discounts for educational or promotional purposes are available. Contact the Publisher for more information.

CONTENTS

Tim Leary & Neal Cassidy on the bus Further

PREFACE

When Ralph & I discussed creating a Seventh volume of Hip Santa Cruz in January, 2024, the first thing we agreed on was that it would be our last issue. Back in 2014 a small group of us set out to test Ralph's theory that psychedelics were driving many of the changes in science, the arts, and society itself. So we recorded interviews with a unique group of psychedelic Pioneers who lived in Santa Cruz from 1960 - 2024, asking each person: How Did You Get to Santa Cruz?, and How have psychedelics affected your life—if at all? We published the oral interviews in 2016 as Hip Santa Cruz.

Word spread, the book stirred interest, and we both started getting calls from other community members eager to share their experiences. We agreed to listen, and the stories came faster than we could print them! By the time we published Hip Santa Cruz #2, we already had enough material for a third issue…and then a fourth, and a fifth!

Twelve years later Ralph and I were both having serious health problems. We already had several stories sitting in a folder on my server for issue #7, and a few other stories were promised and pending. However, old Hippies were fading fast—over a third of those interviewed in our first five volumes have died. Since Ralph and I are Octogenarians, neither one of us knew how long we had left, so we set the "deadline" for submissions to Hip Santa Cruz #7 for Thanksgiving of this year (2024) and sent out the notice to our mailing list.

Little did we know…

The next time I saw Ralph was in June of this year at the Emergency Ward at Dominican Hospital in Santa Cruz. EMT's brought me in due to fainting and collapse caused by sudden blood pressure loss, and heart problems. As they were discharging me, I saw Ralph, unconscious on a gurney, waiting for admission. Over the next few months he was in and out of Dominican Hospital several times. Finally they released him to Hospice home care to Ray Gwyn Smith, Ralph's wife, who was overwhelmed with attending to his needs.

I drove up to see them when he was settled back in their small mountain home. Ralph was barely mobile, flat on his back with his head slightly elevated on a rented hospital bed. Beneath the sheet he was wearing a catheter which he said he was very uncomfortable. He waved his hand to indicate I should sit beside him.

"I want you to take care of the Hip Santa Cruz series. Not all of my books, just the Hip series. You can publish number Seven or not, It's your call. You can use my publisher for the last copy. Hiroko (his secretary) has all the remaining copies of one through six except for the few I have up here. I also have a box of books coming—an order for Bookshop

Santa Cruz. Take charge of that too, refilling the orders as needed. I have other arrangements for my other books..." he sighed and gently squeezed my hand.

"Good. Because taking on any more work at this time of my life would be too much. I'm reaching my limits," I said.

Ralph laughed quietly and smiled for a moment. "Like you, I have limited energy and time, so I think our business is complete, T. Mike. Many people are coming to see me, so I don't think you need to make the journey up here any longer. I feel comfortable about our project. I know you will take care of it."

He sighed. His voice was growing weaker. I squeezed his hand lightly, said goodbye to him for the last time, spoke briefly to Ray on the way out, and hit the winding road back to town.

As you will see, this issue is devoted to Ralph Abraham and his lifetime devotion to uplifting and informing our species' evolving collective mind/conciousness. His work in Math, quantum thinking, Chaos Theory and Fractals, sparked whole systems of thought and helped revolutionize our culture. I am grateful to have known, played, and worked with him.

You hold in your hand the product of a Group Mind, full of stories of lives vividly lived and experienced. It also took many hands and minds to produce this testament, Thank you so much to: Jacob Aman, Andrew Cameron Bailey, Wallace Baine, Bruce Damer, Geoffrey Dunn, Rick Gladstone, Holly Harmon, and Ray Gwyn Smith, for your help creating this issue.

Any typos or spelling errors are my bad.

This Hippy bus will go no Further. We hope this

document will help the next generation find (or create!) a new bus, because "The Road Goes Ever On" (Tolkien)

Ralph & Ray on their return from India, 1972

The Abraham House on California Street, Santa Cruz, CA, 1968 -71

Andrew Cameron Bailey and Ralph Abraham

WELCOME TO PARADISE
By Andrew Cameron Bailey

In the summer of 1969, taking a break from my scientific college-lecturer career in apartheid-era South Africa, I assessed my graduate school option, pursuing a somewhat vague search for something called "cosmic consciousness," I found myself hanging out at the Chelsea College of Art in London, refining my photography skills by volunteering at the studio of Lord Patrick Lichfield - the Royal photographer, best known for his superb fashion and portrait photography. I was deepening my art history education and loving the experience of integrating into a vibrant, world-class city at the very peak of the 1960s. 1969 was a year of widespread student unrest, the Pop Art Retrospective at the Tate, Yoko Ono's "Happening" at the Arts Lab in Drury Lane, the Brian Jones memorial concert in Hyde Park, and Bob Dylan at the Isle of Wight, followed by Woodstock in the USA. The Americans were deeply engaged in a violent and, to my mind, unethical confrontation in Vietnam. A former used-car salesman, Richard Milhouse Nixon, occupied the White House, and a B-grade Hollywood actor named Ronald Reagan had recently been elected Governor of California. The Cold War was in full swing.

There was a strong South African presence in London at the time. Many expats were studying at the famous Chelsea school. Among the English art students were some lovely young women who liked the South African lads, and before I knew it, I was part of a delightful creative community. One of my new female friends learned that my long-term plan was to make my way to California, penniless as I was, and pursue a postgraduate degree there. She introduced me to an American friend of hers, a black American photographer named Reggie Jackson - not the baseball star, needless to say.

Reggie came over to her flat one afternoon, introduced himself, and showed me a striking black-and-white photograph of a bearded, bespectacled man who bore an uncanny resemblance to Jerry Garcia, the iconic lead guitarist of the Grateful Dead. The photograph was not of the famous musician, however, but rather of a mysterious stranger. Reggie explained that the subject of the photograph was Ralph Abraham, PhD, a brilliant American mathematician, a college professor from a place I had never heard of: Santa Cruz, California. Reggie would see if he could arrange an introduction, he said, and we went on to other things, like listening to the latest Rolling Stones album at rafter-shaking volume.

Suddenly, it was a gloomy September afternoon and winter was coming, a phenomenon my sub-tropical upbringing had not prepared me for. Entertaining fantasies of faraway, sunny places, I was meandering along a wet, grimy street in Earl's Court on the way to my temporary crash pad, when I noticed a very attractive girl coming the other way. She was radiantly suntanned - the epitome of an endless summer. I stopped as she turned and went up the steps to a building entrance, then I realized it was my destination as well. I ascended the steps behind her. She turned, smiled and said: Andrew? It was Leslie Anderson, one of the loveliest girls at the Art School in my home town of Durban, South Africa, and like myself, an avid sailor. She was a close friend of my then-sweetheart, Diana Grey, who was still in Cape Town completing her undergraduate degree in philosophy and psychology. Di was due to join me in London as soon as her classes ended.

Les and I stood there on the steps, and my life changed. "What have you been doing? I asked." "Chartering in the Caribbean," she replied. "Really? that would be my ultimate dream, right now." "Are you serious?" She asked. "A friend of mine is looking for crew for a delivery to Granada. Can you meet him at the RORC tomorrow?" "What's the RORC?" "The Royal Ocean Racing Club." And so the adventure began.

As my time in London drew to a close, my art-school friends decided to host a little farewell dinner for me on my last night in the city. They had chosen a peaceful, cozy macrobiotic cafe called Seed, in a side alley away from the bustling streets. It was the perfect spot for an intimate gathering - or so we thought.

We were the only diners. Perfect! We had just settled into our seats, the Eastern music and soft ambience soothing our spirits, when the tranquility was rudely shattered. The restaurant's doors burst open, and in swarmed a boisterous, obnoxious group of stoned Americans, their uncontrolled laughter and uproarious chatter drowning out any chance of serious conversation. They energetically rearranged all the free tables along the wall behind my seat. There must have been fifteen or eighteen of them!

I tried to maintain my composure, even as my annoyance grew. Then, just when it seemed the evening was veering off course, my final guest of the night arrived. It was Reggie Jackson, the photographer. Reggie, an amused glint in his eye, settled into the seat opposite mine, reached across the table to shake my hand, said "Hi!" to Di Gray, who had just arrived in London, and gestured towards the commotion behind me. "Andy," he yelled, leaning closer so I could hear him over the cacophony, "There's Ralph, the man I want you to meet. Come!"

I found myself face to face with the bearded, bespectacled man from Reggie's photograph - Ralph Abraham himself. Ralph extended his hand, introducing himself with a warm smile. Amidst the chaos of the American rowdies, who, by the way, turned out to be Ken Kesey and the Merry Pranksters - of whom I had never heard - Ralph and I managed to exchange a few words. He gave me his contact information in California and told me about his new position at the University of California, Santa Cruz, a brand-new campus. "You'll love it!" he said. He suggested I consider it for my upcoming graduate work, a social anthropological investigation into student unrest. At that moment, I had never heard of UC Santa Cruz, and I had no clue that Santa Cruz, wherever that was, was going to play a pivotal role in my future.

That chance encounter in a London restaurant was the prelude to a journey that took me across the Atlantic to Central

California, to a vibrant little city where the convergence of great surf, redwood trees, art, music, mathematics, and the conscious counterculture would forever change the course of my life. The farewell party at Seed, despite its chaotic start, was the catalyst for a new chapter, one that would be filled with unexpected synchronicities, lifelong friendships, and the exploration of uncharted spiritual territories, in a glorious seaside town on the north shore of Monterey Bay.

The following morning, as the sun was peeking over the London skyline, I bid farewell to the ancient city that had been my home for a brief but significant chapter of my life. With feelings of equal parts excitement and trepidation, I embarked on the first leg of my journey to the New World. Di and I took a train to Gatwick Airport, where I said farewell to my sweetheart and caught a flight to Torino, Italy. Di was welcome to join me on the trans-Atlantic trip, but had decided to remain in London to pursue her art career. We arranged to meet at the World's Fair in Tokyo the following year. It was the last time I ever saw her and I'm still heartbroken.

From Torino, a series of trains and buses took me to the picturesque Mediterranean village of Chiavari. Awaiting me in Chiavari was a sight that would take my breath away - an immaculate, perfectly-restored 90-foot racing yawl, the world's fastest monohull, winner of many prestigious ocean races. I was an experienced sailor, but had never sailed on anything bigger than 52 feet. The owner, one of the Rothschild wine barons, was selling his world-famous Gitana IV to an American millionaire, and our task was to deliver her to Grenada, an island in the West Indies. She gleamed in the late afternoon sun, a vessel of great power, beauty and grace. Beyond the yacht harbor, the Mediterranean Sea beckoned. Vaguely, I realized that I was about to embark on the adventure of a lifetime.

We were in no hurry, and had an unlimited budget. Our entire crew, with the exception of the alcoholic English skipper, was unpaid, but we lived like millionaires. Our course took us westward along the Italian coast to one legendary locale after another, including Portofino, Monaco, Beaulieu, San Tropez and the South of France, the Spanish Costa Brava, Gibraltar, Tangiers, and finally, the Canary Islands, where we moored in an ancient port called Santa Cruz de Tenerife and awaited the official end of hurricane season, October 31st. Santa Cruz! There's that word again. The highlight of our voyage was yet to come, the challenging Atlantic crossing ahead.

It was my first and only ocean crossing. As we plowed deeper into the vastness of the Atlantic, I marveled at the power of the ocean and the resilience of our vessel. We encountered threatening seas and utterly calm waters, torn sails, endless skies, stormy nights and breathtaking sunsets. It was during those solitary moments at the helm in the middle of the night, gazing up at the endless expanse of stars, listening to the breathing of the dolphins alongside, that I felt more alive than at any time in my already adventurous life. I was free!

One of the most memorable experiences of the journey was surfing that mighty 98-ton sailboat into the welcoming waters of Barbados at dawn on November 17th, 1969, my 26th birthday. The thrill of riding those enormous swells on such a grand vessel was a testament to the perfect design of the boat and the skill and expertise of our multi-national crew. As we arrived, I caught a fine, rare wahoo on the fishing line which I towed behind the boat. A better birthday breakfast I could not imagine.

Our voyage culminated in Grenada, where we were met with an uproarious welcome. Every vessel on the island sailed out to greet us! We responded by lining up along the rail, bending over and dropping our pants, in what is apparently called a "brown-out." It wasn't my idea, I swear! The prestigious yacht had garnered attention and admiration wherever we went. As a result, it was at the dock at Grenada Yacht Services that I received news of an opportunity that would change the course of my journey once more.

A job offer awaited me in the United States, one that I couldn't have foreseen when I first boarded that plane in London. The Kennedy yacht, the   notorious Jacqueline herself, was in need of a cook. A cook? WTF? Well, OK. At least it gets me closer to my destination, California. As it turned out, I would be the only one aboard with the skills and knowledge to operate a sailing vessel of this magnitude. I was the fucking cook, but that's a whole 'nother story.! The rest of the crew, I swiftly learned, were retired US Navy personnel. What I did not know was that the US Navy does NOT teach its recruits the most basic rudiments of open-ocean sailing!

Arriving in America on Thanksgiving Day of 1969 with just $45 in my pocket, I felt like a modern-day Mayflower Pilgrim, setting out on an adventure in a land of equal parts danger and opportunity. I sensed that my journey would be filled with unexpected twists and turns, like the pioneers of old, but I was young, immortal and up for anything life might throw at me. I was learning to trust the loving Universe, as it guided me every step of the way.

Joining the crew of the Jacqueline, JFK's personal sailboat, gave me my first taste of American politics. The vessel had recently been sold to a right-wing American millionaire, and the crew, all US Navy-trained, proved to be dangerously incompetent. It was a challenging environment, but I was determined to make the most of it. The Jacqueline had been re-named, absurdly, the Poppsie III and was a monument to the Republican Party, meaning that below decks one waded through 3-inch-deep red-white-and-blue shag carpeting, surrounded by elephants on all sides. Stainless steel ones on the bowsprit and at the mastheads, red ones on the port side, green ones on the starboard, and everything from papier-mâché to bronze to marble elephants everywhere you looked below decks. Very tasteful, I must say.

Our initial charter, over Christmas, took us out to the Bahamas, where the turquoise waters and white sandy beaches provided a stunning backdrop for our charter party's adventures. Despite the crew's shortcomings, I did my best to ensure that our guests had a good time. I enjoy creating memorable experiences for others and I saw myself as the entertainment director.

However, my commitment to the charter party's happiness did not sit well with the yacht's skipper, whose attitude and political leanings clashed just a tiny bit with my own. I was supposed to serve the food and keep my fucking mouth shut. In the end, I found myself without a job, but with a severance payment of fifteen one-hundred dollar bills in my back pocket. A couple of weeks later, my replacement, a gaunt retired US Navy cook, came aboard, I stepped ashore, and Poppsie III sailed off erratically into the sunrise, headed for the US Virgin Islands and a winter season catering to wealthy tourists. With a huge sigh of relief, I watched her disappear into the distance.

Little did I know what I was missing. The vessel was dismasted in a tropical storm off the coast of Cuba, sustaining over $100,000 in avoidable damage. She drifted helplessly for ten miserable days before being captured and towed into Havana by the Cuban navy.

Knowing nothing about the above, but with newfound resources and a strong sense of relief, I set off for the next chapter of my journey, this time with a gorgeous hippie girl named Kendall, my first American girlfriend, by my side. As we drove west toward Los Angeles, stopping in New Orleans for my very first acid trip, I couldn't help wondering about Santa Cruz, a place that had become a beacon of curiosity and fascination ever since my brief encounter with Ralph Abraham in faraway London. Santa Cruz was only three or four hundred miles up the California coast from LA and the prospect of exploring the legendary counterculture scene and intellectual pursuits of San Francisco, just seventy miles to the north, filled me with anticipation. Would I be too late for the Summer of Love?

After spending a couple of weeks in the frenetic City of Angels, it was time to head north. I bid farewell to Kendall and my new friends in LA and hitched a ride to Santa Barbara. From there, I was planning to hitchhike the final leg of my trip to Santa Cruz. I stuck out my thumb at an onramp on Highway 101, praying for a kind soul to offer me a ride. A bright-red VW van screeched to a halt. The driver, a man named Jeff Love, who bore a striking resemblance to the character Ray from the movie "Alice's Restaurant," greeted me with a warm smile.

"What takes you to Santa Cruz?" Jeff asked. Santa Cruz was his destination later that evening, after a quick stop along the way. I couldn't help feeling a sense of serendipity in that moment, as if the universe was once again conspiring to bring me to my destined place at the perfect time. I relaxed and began to enjoy one of the most memorable days of my life.

Jeff described himself as a "psychic entrepreneur" and I began to recount the story of how I had met someone named Ralph Abraham back in London, how our paths had crossed in the most unexpected of ways, and how he had suggested that I consider Santa Cruz for my graduate work. To my astonishment, Jeff's response was: "Ralph Abraham is my business partner!"

The threads of fate seemed to weave themselves together in an intricate but discernible pattern. As we turned off Highway 101 and headed for the coast at Morro Bay, Jeff told me about our destination, its unique spirit, a surfing spot called Steamer Lane, and the groundbreaking project that he and Ralph were involved in together: something called the Pataal Foundation. The Sanskrit word pataal meant the navel or bellybutton of the Universe, he explained. There was a third partner in the venture, an Indian musical guru who lived in London, who was the world's greatest vichitra veena player. His name was Sri Dayal Batish. I had definitely entered another dimension!

I felt an increasing sense of guidance, connection and destiny. By trusting the unknown and putting out my thumb, this "chance" encounter on the road to Santa Cruz would lead to a deep immersion in that city's vibrant culture and the beginning of a new chapter in my life, one that would be forever intertwined with the enigmatic Ralph Abraham and the captivating little city on the California coast.

After a leisurely stop at the Esalen Institute, a place I had never heard of, along the breathtaking Big Sur coast, part of which involved my getting comfortable with being naked in public in the midst of some very beautiful, equally naked women, Jeff Love and I continued our journey northward along the winding highway that led to Santa Cruz. I did not know it yet, but Esalen was about to play a part in my future, as I abandoned academia for the life of a spiritual seeker. I was about to become a graduate school dropout.

The rugged beauty of the California coastline unfurled before us. As the day drew to a close, Jeff offered me a place to stay for the night in a charming redwood mountain town called Boulder Creek. The cozy evening spent on Jeff's couch allowed me to rest and gather my wits, sensing that the next day held the promise of a new beginning.

The following morning, after a brief encounter with a tall, long-haired wizard named Ray Mortz, who gave me two life-transforming books by Teilhard de Chardin and Sri Aurobindo, names that were new to me, I found myself standing on Ralph Abraham's doorstep on California Street in the heart of Santa Cruz. This moment would mark the beginning of a profoundly transformative phase of my life. Ralph, with his deep intellect, resonant voice and magnetic personality, welcomed me into his world with open arms. I gradually discovered that Ralph was at the very heart of the Northern California consciousness scene. He was not only a mathematician but also a bridge between the worlds - connecting the realms of mathematics, spirituality, psychedelics and the emerging counterculture.

Ralph introduced me to some remarkable individuals, leaders who were pushing the boundaries of human understanding and exploration. People like Peter Demma, who was running for County Sheriff on the "legalize marijuana" platform, challenging the status quo in bold and visionary ways. Jazz musician Max Hartstein, with his impassioned pleas for the creation of a neighborhood psychic laboratory, opened my mind to the possibility that everything was already perfect, that we all lived in the Garden of Paradise. "Welcome to Paradise!" he intoned at our first introduction. "Shall I roll another number?" Max got me started in music by inviting me to join his improvisational jazz group, the 25th Century Ensemble, courtesy of which I participated in the creation of some of the strangest music ever heard. It was called "perfect music," perfect because it was no longer possible to hit a wrong note. The group existed in the 25th Century, by which time all the wrong notes had already been played! We improvised every Thursday night at Max's psychic laboratory on the river in Boulder Creek and performed dozens of times to bewildered audiences all up and down the California coast. Every Friday evening we presented a three-hour radio show over the hill in Los Gatos, called The 25th Century Ensemble Hour. It was the most fun I've ever had, to this day. And I've had a lot of fun!

One of the most influential people I encountered through Ralph was Dr. Ralph Metzner, the de-frocked Harvard professor, who initiated me into Agni Yoga, an ancient Hindu meditation practice that resonated deeply with my soul. Other than my early experiments with Zen meditation, it was my first true foray into the world of spirituality, and it marked the beginning of a lifelong journey of self-discovery, inner exploration and sufism.

With each passing day that magical first year, at the Thursday night perfect music sessions, the Friday radio shows, the spring fair and the monthly full-moon festivals, I felt a sense of belonging and purpose that I had never experienced before. I had found my soul tribe, a loving community of creative kindred spirits who shared my thirst for adventure, peace, freedom, knowledge, spiritual growth and above all, FUN. As the years rolled on, Santa Cruz became not merely an interesting place on the map, but my spiritual home. Deeply influenced by a series of Esalen events, including the experience of being Von Neumanized, I decided to drop out of UC Santa Cruz and start my own consciousness research venture, leading ultimately to my PhD. I won't go into the details here, but it was a very educational adventure.

I met my first wife, Blue, at T Mike Walker's memorable 1970/1971 New Year's Eve party. Interestingly, in 1971, I found myself repeating something I had done back in London when I acted as the Royal photographer Pat Lichfield's "gopher," sweeping the floors, mixing chemicals, loading film and running out for snacks and coffee during the shoots. I met Ronald Reagan's personal photographer, Joe Finkelstein. Blue and I started driving up to Sacramento on Fridays and I would spend the night printing hundreds of Reagan photographs, while Joe went off and got laid. Once I got that job done, I was free to use the studio and the darkroom as long as I liked. It is still the best-equipped darkroom I have ever worked in. One lasting legacy: Joe and I set up a shoot with Blue in all her hippie finery with her amazing Johnny Winter hair, and one of those portraits became a famous Tower Records poster. Speaking of posters, Blue was the poster child of the Woodstock festival. Get ahold of the Life magazine Woodstock issue if you can find one. She is the subject of three photos in that issue.

The friends I made during those transformative years of 1970 - 1972 remain some of my closest confidants, companions, and soulmates to this day, including Ralph Abraham himself. I had an hour-long chat with Blue just this morning. Although our marriage ended in 1974, we remain close friends. My Santa Cruz bonds have grown stronger with time, and today, fifty-five years later, Santa Cruz still holds a unique place in my heart - a place where the spirit of adventure, the great music, the intellectual exploration, and the spiritual awakening continue to thrive, just as they did on that fateful January day in 1970 when I knocked on Ralph's California Street door, a pilgrim seeking a new beginning in a beautiful city that will forever be part of my life. Connie and I travel to Santa Cruz pretty much every year, and are always welcomed home as timeless members of a loving, terminally-hip, world-class community.

ADDENDUM: THE ROSS SCHOOL

Ralph Abraham and I stayed in touch regularly from that first fateful meeting in London in September, 1969 until his recent passing in September, 2024. Exactly fifty-five years! In fact, Connie and I were on the road from Colorado to the 40th anniversary of World Peace Day in San Francisco and then on to Santa Cruz to film an interview with Ralph, when we received a sad note from Ray informing us that he had just passed away.

There was a significant phase of Ralph's remarkable life that many of his Santa Cruz friends may be unaware of. My second wife Susan and I had left our home on the San Lorenzo River in Boulder Creek next to Camp Joy in the summer of 1981 with our three little Santa Cruz-born kids in tow. We rented the house to a young couple and took off for New York for a year. At least that was our intention. I had an ambitious plan. This was four years before MTV and I was going to create a television show called Video Top Ten, featuring the world's best music videos. Working with Santa Cruz's Denise Gallant, my young brother Steven and I had had some success with a couple of very early music videos and I was excited. I've always been an excitable boy, and still am! We managed to rent an incredible 11th floor loft in New York City, the top floor and roof garden of 32 Union Square West. Andy Warhol's Factory was on the 6th floor.

That winter, a severe storm hit the Santa Cruz Mountains and did a awful lot of damage. Dozens of people were killed. Dozens of homes were destroyed. Our much loved and renovated house at 12300 Irwin Way, directly across the river from Max's psychic laboratory, was damaged beyond repair. We had to say farewell to about $120,000 in real estate equity, my first-ever financial stash. While we were trying to figure out our next move, thieves came and stole everything of value, and then the Boulder Creek Fire Department came by and torched the place as a fire-fighting exercise. There is nothing there to this day! Thus began our extended New York sojourn. Having no home to return to, we hunkered down in New York, where I had previously lived for years. I knew my way around. This was 1982.

Fast forward a decade or so. Susan and I had traveled out to Santa Cruz for reunions, weddings and so on, and always got together with Ralph if he was in town. On one of those trips, we were staying with Fred and Roberta McPherson in Boulder Creek, and a couple of Fred's friends came over to meet us. Al Lundell and Bruce Damer! They are dear friends to this day. However, we were living in New York and had moved out of the City to the Fabulous Hamptons. We rented an old, drafty farmhouse on 32 acres near the water, had two more kids for a total of five, and I was working in East Hampton as photographer and videographer for an ambitious educational project called the Ross School, named for Steve Ross, the chairman of Time Warner. I hadn't seen much of Ralph in a while. I arrived at work one morning, walked through the lobby and stopped to chat with the receptionist. On her desk was a little pile of books, all by an individual named Ralph Abraham, PhD. "What's up with these books?" I asked. She said, "Oh you know, Courtney's been traveling and she found this guy she wants to work with. He'll be here this afternoon."

Armed with that information, I got to work, leaving my door open. Just as I expected, at some point I heard the elevator door open, and the sound of Ralph's unmistakeable voice. There's no way I could hide my grin, as I stepped out into the hall. Ralph was approaching with my boss, Courtney Sale Ross, universally known a CSR. He looked at me and asked "Andrew! What are you doing here?" I replied, "I work here. What are YOU doing here?"

Thus began a long period in East Hampton where I saw Ralph frequently, and had the privilege of filming, photographing and audio-recording a series of remarkable conferences that he convened in collaboration with some of the most significant thinkers in the world. Below is a brief account of Ralph's twenty-year engagement with Courtney and the Ross Institute. Sadly, Seve Ross, who I really liked, had died of prostate cancer shortly after I started working for the emerging school. In fact, the Ross School began as a home-schooling project at Cody House, their home in East Hampton, so that their little girl Nicole could spend as much time as possible with her dying father. Steven Spielberg was a close neighbor and friend. I got to know him as well. Courtney had become one of the wealthiest women on the planet, up there with the Queen of England. Here's a brief account of Ralph's time with the Institute:

Ralph Abraham's involvement with the Ross Institute and Ross School in New York and East Hampton extended far beyond his mathematical genius. He introduced a wide array of scholars, philosophers, and thinkers to the School and the associated Ross Institute, creating a vibrant intellectual hub. Among those he engaged were notable figures from diverse disciplines, including biologist Rupert Sheldrake and ethnobotanist Terence McKenna, with whom he co-created an influential series at Easalen: Trialogues At The Edge Of The West, Chaos, Creativity, and Cosmic Consciousness. [Do you remember what I left South Africa in search of? Cosmic consciousness. Talk about divine guidance!]

These discussions, which can be found on YouTube, explored the intersections of science, consciousness, and the cosmos, reflecting the Ross Institute's commitment to innovative and interdisciplinary education. Ralph's contributions exemplified his ability to merge chaos theory with cultural and historical insights, inspiring students and educators to see mathematics as a tool to unlock larger truths about the universe, consciousness and existence. His expansive vision drew parallels with his network outside the school, such as his deep involvement in psychedelic research, which he believed could offer profound perspectives on the "Big Picture" of reality.

Among the notable intellectuals who visited Ross through Ralph's influence were figures like Gregory Bateson, a systems theorist who was key in developing interdisciplinary approaches to biology, psychology, and culture; Lynn Margulis, whose groundbreaking work in biology revolutionized our understanding of evolution; James Lovelock, who introduced the Gaia hypothesis, seeing Earth as a self-regulating system; and David Spangler, a spiritual teacher and author. These thinkers shared Abraham's commitment to transforming education and society by merging scientific inquiry with spiritual and philosophical exploration. People like Riane Eisler, David Fiedler, Joan Halifax and many more, were frequent contributors.

His network included luminaries from Lindisfarne, a community founded by William Irwin Thompson, who, along with E.F. Schumacher (author of Small is Beautiful), Hazel Henderson, and Brother David Steindl-Rast, all contributed to the intellectual currents that he brought to Ross. These individuals brought diverse perspectives, from ecological economics to feminist archeology to spiritual practice, enriching the intellectual environment at Ross. The Ross students were the recipients of a most extraordinary education, and Ralph had a lot to do with that

The Ross Institute's work, deeply influenced by Ralph

and his associates, continues to resonate in contemporary conversations about education, sustainability, and cultural transformation, emphasizing the integration of knowledge across disciplines to create a more holistic view of the world.

CLOSING NOTE

I'd like to end with a few personal historical notes and a couple of suggestions. As a 14-year old South African schoolboy in a rather fine boy's high school called Glenwood High, I was exposed to a powerful influence, Zen Buddhism. A small group of us became intrigued at the possibilities of Zen meditation. We were inspired by the writings of an Anglo-Tibetan author named Lobsang Rampa and his descriptions of flying monks and other miracles. We were hooked! At the same time we were passing around Jack Kerouac's controversial book On The Road. By the time The Dharma Bums was published, some of us were ready to get on the road ourselves. Especially yours truly! I didn't know it yet, but I was headed for Neil Cassidy's home town, Santa Cruz, CA.

In Santa Cruz, one of the first people I bonded with was Leon Tabory, at the the Flower Farm commune in La Selva Beach. My favorite Leon quote is: "The Hippies had it right all along!" Jesus Christ was the original hippie, so I'd like to close with a word of caution about the so-called "Christians" currently taking over America. White Christian nationalism rapidly leads to authoritarianism and ultimately Nazism. I know what I'm talking about, having grown up in South Africa where the name of the ruling Afrikaner party was pronounced "Die Nazi-oh-nale Part-ay." Its Dutch Calvinist leaders were real life pro-Hitler Nazis who spent WWII in internship camps. In English, "Nazi-oh-nale" translates simply as "Nationalist."

In today's increasingly terrifying version of Amerika, it's not unreasonable to wonder whether the Fourth Reich is beginning it's ugly reign as it takes over the White House.

It might be time to read, or re-read, a book called The Rise And Fall Of The Third Reich. I read it at age fourteen and was severely nauseated for years as a result. I still am, come to think of it. On a related subject, may I recommend The Rise And Fall Of The Zulu Empire? It's not as nauseating as the one about the Nazis, but it does take a strong stomach.

Those future prime ministers of South Africa lived by a mantra you may have heard:"Deutschland über Alles" - which translates to "Germany above Everything" in English. Adolf Hitler's political party was the National Socialist German Workers' Party. It is commonly referred to as the Nazi Party. The current American version is "America First." You have been warned! We Americans need to wake up, be woke and proud of our wokeness! "Woke" means awake. The word "hip" means "aware" or"conscious" as in "I'm hip, man!" It comes from the West African term "hipicat" which translates as "an elegant, conscious, well-educated person." So, dear hippies, we had it right all along. We are elegant, conscious, well-educated people and always have been.

Finally, if any of you are feeling, as I am, profoundly hopeless and helpless these days, here are two suggestions for the 2/3rds of Americans who did not vote for Trump. First, we are anything but powerless. We have an immense ability to influence the future, and it's not illegal. It's called the power of the pocket book. A boycott movement is getting underway, and you can start right now, with your very next purchase! Consider this: As of 2024, the estimated population of the United States is approximately 345 million people. Two-thirds of that number is 230 million. If We the People, or 2/3rds of us at least, were to commit to withholding just $10 per month, ideally much more, from the right-wing businesses and individuals that control and support the incoming regime, and re-direct our purchases to ethical entities such as the thousands of mom and pop enterprises and small family farmers (the true Americans if you will) that Walmart and Big Ag forced out of business, what would the financial impact be? $2,300,000,000 per month. $2,3 billion dollars. Every month! Annually, that adds up to $27,600,000,000, $27.6 billion per year. Ouch! That would hit certain people where it hurts. It might just persuade a few billionaires to try a little wokeness themselves? What if an evolutionary wakeup occurred?

There's quite a list of potential targets for the boycott, starting with my once-respected countryman Elon Musk. Get rid of your Tesla. There are many amazing EV alternatives. Dump your Tesla stock. Get off "X" and move to Bluesky, if you haven't already. There are plenty of better, more human, more climate-friendly sources for everything you need, wherever you spend your hard-earned money. Amazon isn't one of them, I don't think. I will personally never set foot in a Walmart again. Or the right-wing "Christian" chain Hobby Lobby (they don't serve Jews.) I will never use a U-Line product. U-Line is the multi-billion dollar brainchild of a German Nazi family that has one mission in life: the total destruction of American democracy. The list goes on. Do your homework. Make your own list.Tell your friends. Research where your money goes. Is your bank an ethical entity? Together, we CAN make a difference!

Most importantly, TRUST THE LOVING UNIVERSE! We are spirits in temporary human bodies. The Universe has our backs. This too shall pass!

Farewell Ralph, my dear brother, friend and mentor. See you on the other side! For myself, I'm seriously considering moving back to the southern hemisphere, to a land down under. The Australian Aborigines have invited us to come and live with them. We might just take them up on the offer! At 81 years of age, this old hippie is ready for his next adventure.

Andrew C. Bailey, Ralph A. And Connie Baxter Marlow

RALPH ABRAHAM — FIRST MEETING
By Rick Gladstone

On a gray, rainy winter morning in 1969, in a lovely seaside town on the central coast of California, I sat reading, ensconced in a familiar, welcoming, bone-warming café/delicatessen named the Catalyst, located in the grand carriage room of a 19th century hotel. Bathed in the scents of heated cinnamon buns and roasted coffee, I was only dimly aware of the occasional squalls of a pacific storm gathering strength outside; seagulls whooshing by on accelerated glides; ceiling-high windows with paisley-like shimmering tumbling rivulets, a water-colored world washed with rain.

The large yet oddly intimate room was mostly full, as it often would be on wet days in an otherwise sunny climate that biogeographers would later come to term as "Mediterranean", one of only a half-dozen similar "blue" zones on planet Earth. The mostly longhaired, counter-culture folk who frequented the place - some with children in tow - were sitting at tables exchanging information on weather conditions from up in the mountains or employment opportunities, maybe playing chess or backgammon. Some "cool" west-coast jazz was playing soft and low.

I was deeply engrossed in my book, but sensed a presence, and looking up was surprised to see a gentleman standing a few feet away, a cup of coffee in one hand and some literature tucked under the other arm, gazing around the room. He appeared youngish, maybe ten years older than me. He had a head of dark, wavy, shoulder-length hair, the makings of a beard beneath twinkling eyes and was wearing a green, zippered jacket and waterproof boots. As I awkwardly shifted from the fantastical world of my book to the present moment, I felt that vague unease of knowing this person but not quite able to identify the face or voice. He turned slightly and spoke to me.

"Most of the tables are full or taken. Mind if I join you?"

Normally, given my somewhat solitary nature, I would have begun to panic just a little, but in this case felt no such need. I waved at the seat across from me and he sat down, laying a couple of journal like publications on the table, face down. I wondered, as a book store/library habitué, about their contents, but was too shy to ask.

He offered his hand. "My name is Ralph."

I extended mine and felt his firm and thankfully unaggressive squeeze. "I'm Rick."

Small smiles. His face was very familiar to me, but I was sure we had never met. If nothing else, he reminded me of a couple of relatives, an uncle or maybe a cousin, from my mom's side of the family. I asked him if he came into the Catalyst very often, mentioned that I did and wasn't sure if I'd seen him before.

"Not too often, but more lately."

I asked the perfunctory question among the morning regulars: "Are you looking for work?"

He laughed, a great smile, very amused. "No, I've got a pretty good job."

His tone, I felt, left room for interpretation. I wanted to know what kind of work allowed him to be in the Catalyst at eleven in the morning. But being primarily a local myself, one who is occasionally employed but always looking for part-time or temporary day-labor work, I couldn't bring myself to broach the subject, sort of a defensive, self-censoring, class-consciousness. Ralph might have sensed my unease.

"What are you reading?"

I may have blushed a bit. Suddenly it felt a couple of

degrees warmer in the café. Now I was on the spot. I would have to divulge part of my little secret, a private world I had been exploring since grade school.,"Um, it's just a book I found recently in the New Discovery used bookstore in North Beach up in The City." I showed him the cover that read, Cosmic Humanism, by Oliver Reiser.

"Oh, yes, I know Oliver," Ralph exclaimed." I just read it a couple of months ago."

I sat a moment in stunned silence. "How do you know of Reiser?"

"Well, I'm a professor of math up at the university. But I met Oliver at a conference back east when I was teaching at Princeton."

This made sense. Reiser was a professor at University of Pittsburg. Ralph sipped his coffee and peered at me. "So, what's your interest in Reiser?"

I told him I had been following a path since childhood that had led me to examine systems theory, entropy and trophic systems in biology and society. "Reiser appears to see all things as connected. That's not bad for a western philosopher. He describes material reality as "harmonic nodes in a sea of electrical density". I like that, but I've adapted the phrase. I'm a musician. I view it as harmonic nodes in a sea of vibrational density."

Ralph smiled.

Over the next hour or so we talked. Ralph described his interest and research in dynamic and non-linear systems. I felt a charge of excitement, the sort of sensation I recognized whenever I had randomly met someone who was a fellow traveler or explorer, and way out ahead of me on that road to boot. He told me he had been experimenting with psychoactive substances and was interested in the evolution and process of consciousness. I mentioned I had first taken

LSD in 1963 when I was 15, going into my junior year in high school. He was interested to know about my experience.

When we were finished and got ready to go the rain had subsided and the sun was peaking through the clouds. The Catalyst morning-folks had morphed into the lunch crowd. Ralph asked if I was having any luck finding work. Not much, I told him, but I had plans to start another newspaper. He asked about it and I told him it was to be a collective effort, an "alternative press", hopefully a Santa Cruz original. He thought for a moment. "Maybe I could contribute something."

"Oh, for sure! Send me what you've got or drop it by the house. We hope to get an office downtown if things work out." I wrote down our address on a napkin. And so began The Free Spaghetti Dinner's run as publisher of Ralph Abraham's fascinating column "Scientific Advice on the Politics of Life." And, of course, written under the nom de plume of Dr. Abraham Clearquill.

Later, recounting my experience to housemates after dinner, one remarked: "Oh, I know who he is; a Math professor with dark curly hair named Abraham. He was in the news last year, got in trouble at an anti-Vietnam protest up on the campus. Wore a shirt made from an American Flag. All the warmongers had a cow. He and that other Prof, Paul Lee, I think."

Zap! That was him - the guy whose face I sort of recognized but couldn't put a name to. In1968 I was living in Berkeley, a student at Cal. I'd caught a glimpse of the news photo and had recognized Dr. Lee, whom I knew. He was a professor who had come to teach at UCSC two years before Ralph and had written a couple of articles for the first paper I'd co-published with Tom Scribner and John Tuck in 1967, The Redwood Ripsaw. All things connected.

I saw Ralph rarely in the intervening decades between

1971 and 2014. I was knee deep in work and family, and rarely got out and about. I worked long hours for fifteen years in the computer industry and then for fifteen years in local school districts. However, I had continued to pursue my own course of inquiry, leveraging a life-long desire to subvert the capitalist paradigm and a base of non-linearity and complex systems into the realm of ecological and steady state economics. Still, it seemed, at least once every couple of years Ralph and I would run into each other, catch up and then carry on our respective ways.

What amazed me was how much of what I was reading resonated with Ralph's researches. Not so much in the consciousness field – though I did consider that to be always present as an emergent local property in a generalized cosmic field - but in non-linear and dynamic systems. Many of the books I had read were very familiar to Ralph and quite often he knew and/or worked with the authors: René Tom, Immanuel Wallerstein, Benoit Mandelbrot, Jay Forrester, William Irwin Thompson, Kenneth Boulding, Gregory Bateson, Ludwig von Bertalanffy, etc. One day, in the mid-aughts, while doing some research on curriculum enrichment for secondary education, I came across the Hip History story-circle web site. I recognized and knew most of the people sitting around the table in the picture. A lot of memories bubbled up. Ten years later a dear pal from our late teens, Lex van Zyl, called to tell me he'd run into Ralph who mentioned the Hip History book project and had asked him for my contact info. Ralph emailed me to ask for an interview. We met in a café on the West Side. I told Ralph that this felt like a kind of entanglement.

I was thankfully accompanied to the Hip History Volume 1 book launch at the Blitzer Gallery by my dear wife Karen, my oldest Santa Cruz buddy, Professor Gene Moriarty and our daughter's God-mother Dr. Mischa Adams, all there for moral support as Ralph had asked me to be the first speaker. I was able to introduce Ralph to Mischa. They shared a deep connection to Gregory Bateson, who had been one of Mischa's mentors and thesis advisors, as well as a friend and colleague of Ralph's. And, as the chaos of life would have it, Gregory was a personal friend of my family and mine.

During the evening Ralph and Gene were able to reconnect after thirty years. Gene had often asked about Ralph and his work and I encouraged him to visit Ralph on campus. But Gene was pretty booked up as a professor of Electrical Engineering plus his side-gig, teaching ethics classes for computer engineering students, at San Jose State. One day in the mid-80s, at my prompting and conveying my greetings, Gene went up to Ralph's office and introduced himself. Ralph later began chapter one of Chaos Gaia Eros with the results of that meeting. At the end of the book launch Ralph said we should all keep in touch. He proposed that he, Gene and I should get together for lunch. A couple of months later we did and that began a regular lunch date, two to three times a year for the next eight years.

Ralph and Gene had some things in common: Both had BSc degrees in Mathematical Physics and graduate degrees in Electrical Engineering. Both had a deep interest in metaphysics and both mentored a generation of successful scientists, engineers and mathematicians. Both had written or co authored textbooks of non-linear math and engaged in research on various types of non-linear systems. It has been one of the great pleasures and honors of my life to hang out with those two guys, sitting out on the back patio of the Crepe Place, asking questions, swapping stories, ideas and dreams and rocking in the realm of the episteme.

Other things I cherish about Ralph:

His love for and devotion to his wife and life partner, the

marvelous artist Ray Gwyn Smith.

His ham radio expertise: He developed it as a kid recovering from a frightful illness sustained in early adolescence that kept him out of school for two years. After the Santa Cruz Mountains fire which threatened his and Ray's home he busted it out and plugged into an early warning network with like-minded operators. [This turned out to be another odd connection. I suffered a life-threatening liver disease at six years old. I missed the whole second grade, which turned out to be the single best year of education in my life until I got to college. I was not a very good student, but the weekly visits I received from the district tutor, while quarantined in our housing project apartment in San Francisco, sustained me for the next ten years.]

His covert, card shark persona: Ralph, da' Jack o' Hearts!

His love of hard-bop jazz: I said he was planning a book about it.

His love of teaching, both at university and the Ross School: the world's least appreciated but most admirable profession. Those who understand Buddhist ideas of education and learning, or the Marxist idea of social reproduction, get that. Those who see it as an annoying expense, or a for-profit industry, don't.

I asked Ralph about his ancestry. He told us he had used one of the services on the market, 23 and Me, etc. "What did you learn?"

"Ninety-eight percent Ashkenazi. Boring!" He replied.

I mentioned I'd read about genetic markers that point towards a central Asian origin for some groups within the Ashkenazi. It is somewhat of a fringe theory, I told him, but he found the idea encouraging.

The fact that we were both in Amsterdam at the same

time: This was during what Ralph termed "My miracle year, 1972" in his book Demystifying the Akasha. Ralph was teaching catastrophe theory at the University of Amsterdam, on his way eventually to India by summer. I was living on the streets, trying to avoid catastrophe, while conserving my funds for the leg of my journey in June to Stockholm. Ralph ran into an old friend of his, Baba Ram Das, which set in motion his amazing trip to Nainital, one that had a profound effect on his life.

We also determined that both of us were living in Berkeley during the mad, mad summer of '68, Ralph was conferring with colleagues, and I was going to school, working and up to my neck in some intense political activity.

And right now I'm thinking of Ralph Abraham and the fractal nature of experience. And what I think is: "Ralph, your contribution to the world is wide and deep, profound and boundless. What a mensch!"

Rick Gladstone in the Carriage Room of the Original Catalyst, 1969

MEMORIES OF THE SANTA CRUZ FOOD CO-OP/COMMUNITY FOODS
A Group Writing

This reminder of the Santa Cruz Co-op years will bring back memories for some and hopefully remind us all of how lucky we are to live in a town with so many good food stores, who have histories of their own. Our voices may overlap with information, but we give voice to some of those who were there and remember. These memories have been compiled by Allen Bernklau, Bob Intersimone, Alayne Meeks, Kenny Welcher, and Mary Young.

OPENING THOUGHTS BY ALAYNE MEEKS

In 1970, David Meeks wrote an article for the free weekly newspaper The Free Spaghetti Dinner, a predecessor of the Good Times. David described the benefits of the Berkeley Food Co-op, whose membership entitled shoppers to receive dividends back at the end of the year based on their shopping record. Santa Cruz, according to David, was ready for such a store.

This article drew Bob Intersimone, from Bonny Doon, and Ron and Kelly Barnett, who ran the Dead Cow at the Tannery and who were already discussing creating a buying club, to meet with David at his down shop Custom Alpine Equipment Store on River St. They went to a buying club meeting at the Barnett home in Aptos, where the first bags of food were brought. This location was quickly outgrown by the success of the club. Luckily, in back of David's business, there was a warehouse on North Pacific just before the entrance to the Heart of Santa Cruz Mobile Home Park and across from the

El Dorado Meat Locker where Lenz Arts now resides. In the warehouse was a surfboard fin shop that rented only part of the building. In the front was an office space with an outside door, a sliding window to an office space inside, and enough room to hold a barrel of honey and bags of dry goods. The buying club quickly morphed into a Food Co-op.

David and Bob shared duties of the checkbook while volunteers opened and monitored the division of food, but it was becoming more obvious that this was rapidly becoming a full time business needing a consistency of workers. But it was also being run as a co-op where people paid $5/year to join, and where their purchases were recorded so they could be paid a dividend. We were happy, naïve, struggling, learning, and eating watermelons during the meetings in the Co-op parking lot.

Following is the only newsletter I still have a copy of that was probably written by Bob Intersimone in 1972. It's hard to believe how much happened in the Co-op's first year.

CO-OP NEWSLETTER: NUMBER ONE
After the Winter Solstice, 1972

A Short History of the Co-op

This is our first newsletter, the first of a series which will be appearing monthly (or so). Because many of you will be interested, and in order to give you some perspective, we are going to begin by briefly describing the history of the Co-op.

It began as a buying club, involving 20 or so families. Just as that began to falter, Dave Meeks said that he would take it over. That very same week Bob Intersimone began to organize a co-op, met Dave and some other folks, and we started. We "officially" began on January 1, 1971, so we are just now celebrating our first anniversary.

At first the Co-op was open Saturdays only, but the volume doubled every month, forcing it to be open more and more days each week. We wanted it to be small but it kept growing. Simultaneously, we were selling refundable memberships at $5.00 each, with the understanding that all money taken in over expenses would be refunded to the members in proportion to the amount of their purchases over a 6 month period.

Growth inevitably brought the need for someone to keep it together--a paid manager, and later, more employees in the form of day managers to oversee individual days. Most of our checking has been done by volunteers, and volunteers have also done some trucking, cleaning, building, etc. The energy, morale, and lowness of food prices at the Co-op are in direct correlation to the amount of volunteer help, particularly in checking. More on this later.

The Great Change

We heard from some folks who had done another co-op that unless we were legally incorporated and registered with the state Dave and Bob could be in much trouble. The heavy danger: they had signed all the business papers, meaning that they could be termed "partners," thus causing us technically not to be a co-op.

We found that running the place as a co-op was not enough for the law, while in order to become a legally incorporated co-op one needs $6,000-$10,000 in the bank in the form of $10 memberships in advance of opening, not to mention many other legal and psychic hassles. No one was willing to go through it.

Long discussions at two successive general membership

meetings followed, trying to figure out the best alternative. The decision was to become a non profit corporation. Rather than incorporate ourselves, requiring time and money, etc., we affiliated with University Services Agency, an independent non-profit corporation with which the Whole Earth Restaurant and the Switchboard are affiliated. It means that we use their legal identity so that we don't pay taxes while at the same time Dave and Bob are free of personal responsibility.

USA exerts no pressure on us, and in fact there is a clause in our by-laws that we can disaffiliate from them at any time. We have a representative (Bob) on the USA board, and thus have communication with the Whole Earth Restaurant, Switchboard, and other groups which have affiliated.

The Co-op Here and Now

In order to assume the new legal status we must refund all of the $5.00 memberships and close out the old books. Which brings us to a discussion of the financial condition of the Co-op. A number of membership refunds have already been made--in fact, after "The Big Change" was decided upon, many refunds were given back so quickly that our financial scene is turning out to be very tight. Consequently, we cannot give back too many at once. In addition, we will give to each member a 10% dividend on his or her first six months purchases, but as we are not a legal co-op we cannot give further dividends.

Looking at more specific aspects of our financial condition: the report given at the membership meeting before last was based on miscalculations. At that point the Co-op had $2500 in the bank and an estimated inventory of $2500. Another inventory just completed shows closer to $4000 in stock (to cover the increases in sales volume). Simultaneously, the folks in the membership are owed between $3000 and $4000 in refunds and dividends. It doesn't take a heavy mind to see that this means that the Co-op is not overly affluent. Two immediate steps seem self-evident: 1) membership refunds can be mailed out only a few at a time; 2) all of you are encouraged to reinvest your refunds in the co-op (perhaps gifts, loans, etc.). The "extra" 10% over expenses (900/mo.) will enable us to return all money owed in about 6 months. After that time there should be a surplus.

We recognize that the technical change from a membership co-op to a non-profit organization has caused some confusion and, in some cases, even some loss of confidence in the Co-op. Folks who didn't make it to the important meetings where those long discussions took place leading up to the change have had to find out what happened by word of mouth, the grapevine, from checkers--often quickly in passing. We regret any negative vibrations coming from this. This kind of communication problem is one of the reasons that this newsletter has been started, and why it is important for the folks to come to the general meetings.

On the current day-by-day basis the Co-op is doing well. There are many new items and the sales volume is up to $9000 per month. The Co-op is open the most days ever now, too: Tuesday through Saturday of each week.

Volunteers

As we said earlier, the energy, morale, and lowness of food prices are in direct correlation to the amount of volunteer help. This is a fundamental principle of our Co-op, and is one of the reasons that many of us joined. The Co-op offered another space in our lives in which we could directly participate and have some personal impact on--a space that had the values of a new consciousness. In this case it has to do with the food we eat and the whole atmosphere surrounding obtaining it. The truth is, though, that it has become increasingly difficult to get the volunteers. It is more a complicated and demanding job than it used to be, true, but even so any alert person can handle it. There seems to be an attitude by some: "this place is working fine by itself and it's so big that it doesn't need me." That is not true. We--all of us--are the Co-op, and from us come the volunteers. In the past the volunteer situation has been anarchistic--people coming and helping whenever they had time. Now, however, we also want to go in the direction of regular, reliable volunteers--people who will commit themselves to a regular segment of time each week, from one hour to several hours. Some people are doing this already. Can you? Please come in and sign up at the Co-op.

Board of Directors

The Co-op must elect a board of directors. They will be selected at the next general meeting, which will be Saturday, Jan. 22, at 3:00 P.M. at the Co-op. It will be a working board and anyone wishing to be a part of it should be sure to be at the next general meeting. General meetings, by the way, will be getting together once a month.

The kind of news you don't like to have to report

We will end with a brief note on our saddest problem to date. There is evidence that some folks are taking advantage of our trust. Using the term "ripping off" sounds harsh in the context of the Co-op's atmosphere, but there is evidence…In other words, we are all being hurt financially (and mentally) by a few inconsiderate people. If any of us see this happening we must at least explain that this kind of action hurts us all."

2023 CO-OP MEMORIES OF ROBERT (BOB) INTERSIMONE

The beginning

As a buying club, several of us took turns driving up to Bay Area wholesale food suppliers, such as Pacific Distributors and brought back bags and boxes of dry goods. Then, we would meet on Saturday morning to divide up the bulk foods into our individual orders. We had the use of a small room in a warehouse on North Pacific Street, where we stored the food until it could be divided up and also stored any surplus for future orders.

Organic growth

We were only intending to have a small group, but it did not take long for the word to spread that some people, us, had found a way to get bulk natural foods at wholesale prices. At that time, the only sources for organic or natural foods for most people were local, high-priced health food stores.

I remember one Saturday, after we finished dividing up our orders, we opened the door and there was a small crowd gathered outside. They asked, "Do you have cheap natural foods here? Can we buy some?"

Our core group had to retreat into our little room and discuss this and we decided, "Why not?" We could sell our surplus food at 20% over our wholesale cost and the revenue would help pay for our gas going to San Francisco and back.

Also, with more people wanting food we could order more types of products. So we decided to open the door to the small group gathered on the sidewalk - not imagining that group would soon grow to be large numbers of people.

The Co-op was not a traditional store "selling" to the public. We were just people buying food together as efficiently as possible. In fact, we did not even have a sign on our building for several months, but our volume doubled every month. As luck would have it, the other tenant of the warehouse moved out and we were able to move back into the warehouse in stages until fairly soon, we occupied the whole space.

Even though this was a lot more work than we anticipated, it was a very exciting time. We listened to requests of what people wanted and people were not hesitant to tell us! So we kept expanding our offerings into more and more lines of food until we had a whole warehouse full of beans, grains, nuts, dried fruit, and all kinds of non-perishable bulk items.

In a way, we were Costco before Costco. We had a no-frills warehouse, and we bought food in the largest bulk we could, big 100 pound bags and 50 pound drums, but with one key difference from Costco as it now exists. The buyers of the food could get as little or as much as they wanted and they still got the advantage of bulk buying without a big markup. The one disadvantage of this set-up was that every single bag needed to be weighed, so check out was a little bit time consuming.

We gradually expanded our hours, and days, from Saturday to Friday and Saturday, to Thursday. Friday, Saturday until it did not take long to be open seven days a week, which allowed us to stock perishable foods and produce.

I managed the operations and Dave Meeks managed the business side. I think I was the first paid employee. As I recall,

I got the princely sum of $200 a month plus all I could eat. I believe Dave Meeks did not take any compensation for his tremendous work managing the business and bookkeeping aspects.

The spirit of service

This kind of operation could only exist because of the goodwill and labor of our members and contributions of other people in the community. For example, as their contribution to the Co op, John and Nancy Lengerman offered to let me build a small yurt on their property and live there rent free. We had many wonderful volunteers, some of whom went well beyond what they were asked to do. I want to especially mention Bo Forsyth, who took on the responsibility of keeping the warehouse in order. This was a huge task, because as you can imagine, our members constantly spilled beans and grains and fruits and everything else as they were loading up their individual bags. Bo's wife Elissa used to clean the bathroom and leave a fresh bouquet of flowers on the back of the toilet. It was a lot of work and took several people to keep the warehouse clean and organized. When the health department eventually discovered our little, out-of-the-way food business, because of this great work of Bo and the other volunteers, they did not shut us down, but they did require us to start to provide bins instead of just open bags and boxes. These examples of loving service made the Co-op a wonderful experience for everyone in the community.

We gradually expanded our offerings, again with wonderful contributions from the community, People figured out how to rig up a 55 gallon drum with a heater to dispense honey and racks to accommodate oils and all kinds of other creative solutions. We had regular meetings of the membership and had many spirited discussions about what foods to offer. People had strong opinions about this. I remember the people who followed the Arnold Ehret Mucus-less Diet wanted to offer only fruits and vegetables and perhaps a few nuts. The macrobiotic people wanted grains and some vegetables - limited fruits. The protein people loudly requested cheese and milk products. We even had a bee pollen guy, who gently suggested that all we needed was bee pollen and a couple of other superfood powders and that's all that would be required for optimum human health.

I remember one meeting in particular, where everyone was having a heated discussion about the various benefits and detriments of these different diets. I looked around and it occurred to me, "You all look pretty healthy. Maybe all of these diets are OK as long as they have natural foods." (Of course, it didn't hurt that almost all the members were in their 20s and 30s.) So, it was decided that we would stock all kinds of plant-based, natural whole foods.

We became a great outlet for all the organic growers in the area. It was wonderful how different local people growing organic food started showing up and we just bought everything they brought in. We made a decision early on to only offer whole natural foods and not get into processed foods, vitamins and other packaged goods that the health food stores needed to sell to survive. So you might say that we were a real Whole Foods store before the stores that now call themselves Whole Foods.

This was another contentious issue, because some people really wanted the discounts on processed foods while other people felt to offer those would be going too far away from our core values. Of course, over time because of member demand, these things were gradually added to the offerings.

Unexpected partners

More and more creativity expanded out from the Co-op further and further into the Santa Cruz community and beyond. For example, people who lived on an abandoned pear orchard offered pears to us if we could pick them. Those pears had surface imperfections and were deemed not suitable for commercial sales. So, basically the pears were ours for free just to clean up the orchard. We hired a bunch of hippies to pick them for 5 cents a pound and we sold them for 8 cents a pound. Needless to say, that large crop sold out very quickly. Another friend had a grandfather with an apricot orchard right in the middle of what is now a Silicon Valley shopping center, and we got a group together and went over there and picked apricots. The same thing happened with apples and all kinds of other crops.

A man who was very passionate about farming and supporting small farmers suggested he could bring citrus from the Central Valley and almonds and other crops. We were more than happy to have him do that. We were one of the first stores I know of to do farmer-to-consumer with as little middleman cost as possible.

Then, we started to source internationally. One of my friends had a connection in Mexico and decided to import bananas, tomatoes, avocados, and other things. Unfortunately, his old flatbed truck broke down fairly often in the desert on the way home. He would arrive several days late, throw the tarp off of the back of the truck and a cloud of fruit flies would burst into the air from his truckload of mostly rotting fruit. But even he succeeded eventually. One time, when he broke down near the town of Indio, some people who were living at a small abandoned date orchard took him in. They had picked these organic dates and were selling them at a roadside stand. My friend bought up all the dates they had and brought them up to the Co op. Long-story-short, he became the organic date king of Indio and the Coachella Valley, bringing up and wholesaling tons of dates.

Partnering with other businesses

We also had wonderful cooperation with other businesses just starting in Santa Cruz. Harmony Foods made Mount Kilimanjaro Muesli and also started selling the individual ingredients. They were one of the first ones to put bins of bulk natural foods in markets. We partnered with them to buy food in larger quantities to get greater discounts. We did the same with Staff of Life Bakery, which started out as several people rolling dough by hand - a very small operation - and grew to be a very successful wholesale and retail bakery, and may be one of the last locally owned natural food store in Santa Cruz County.

We also had informal partnerships with other companies such as Westbrae Market of Berkeley. We cooperated in sourcing cheap or free fruit and they had groups of people, who would dry that fruit and produce other products such as apple juice.

A group of our members pointed out that there was quite a population of members up in the Felton/Big Basin area and suggested they open a branch up there. We were happy to accommodate them, order food with them and help make that happen.

Over time, we became one of the biggest sellers of natural foods by volume in the Bay Area. People would come from Mendocino in the north, from Nevada City in the east, from Monterey in the South and lots of other places to buy at our little Co-op. We actually sold food in bulk packaging, such as bulk bags of rice, at 10% over cost. It was a wonderful time providing whole natural foods to the greater community of Northern California.

Outgrowing our "buying club" phase

As we grew, it became obvious that we were becoming a real business, not just a group of people buying food. We researched becoming an official co-op, which would cost a lot of money and involve a lot of legal paperwork and none of us felt like we wanted to go that route. So, we affiliated with University Services Agency (USA), an umbrella nonprofit organization founded at UCSC.Since Dave Meeks and I were the legal owners, we sold out to the new legal entity for $1, which I think was a real bargain, and we ceremoniously tore the dollar bill in half each, retaining a piece.

Beyond the food store

Being affiliated with USA gave several people ideas of other things that could be brought under this umbrella. Tom and Patty Dunks merged The Way of Life herb and tea shop with the food Co-op. The Grover brothers, Tom Robinson, and I started General Hardware and Feed for mail-order hardware, animal feed and gardening supplies in a big old barn down by 41st Avenue, which became a big hit and is still in business today as General Feed and Seed.

The failed greater vision

All this activity caught the attention of some people affiliated with the Whole Earth Catalog over in Menlo Park. They suggested we form a People's Bank, which would pay no interest to depositors and would use the deposited funds as seed money for more nonprofit businesses, with the eventual goal of making Santa Cruz a nonprofit city.

We got immediate pushback from a couple of members of the board of USA. For example, one man, who owned the local for-profit bookshop, was not thrilled with the idea of a new nonprofit bookshop down the street.

We had a meeting and presented the idea to the Co-op population and were surprised at the negative responses we got. We proposed adding something like a 2% surcharge to everything bought at all the nonprofit organizations affiliated with the bank, which would fund the operation of the bank. Our members pretty much overwhelmingly rejected the idea. Some people said it was adding too much unnecessary bureaucracy. Others said that you could not trust anybody who does a bank; other people objected that people from out of town would be in charge, etc.

The number of objections and, from my point of view, the lack of vision, was really disappointing. I believe this was the start of the demise of the Co-op in its early incarnation. Most of the people seemed quite happy to have us work really hard, have volunteers contribute their efforts and provide cheap food, hardware and feed and anything else we could think of, but they were not willing to participate or contribute to the greater vision. That is why the evolution of the Co-op to a worker-owned business was probably the right direction. I must say, I became disillusioned with the community and eventually moved away and started a smaller co-op in Carmel Valley.

The Santa Cruz Food Co-op's founding time was now over and it began a move towards the next phase of its business life

Once its time at North Pacific was done, and I don't remember why the move was made, the Co-op moved into the old Staff of Life building on Seabright vacated when Staff moved to Water Street. The Seabright Brewery now stands where those buildings once were. The year was around 1974 and the Co-op stayed there until the late '70s when they moved to Commercial Way in back of the old Carhart Rental property. Way of Life also became a part of USA and began sharing building space with the Co-op at this time.

Santa Cruz Co-op (Community Foods) on Commercial Way by Kenny Welcher

I began with Community Foods back in the summer of 1978, it was located on Commercial Way then, behind Carhart Rentals. There were three of us "summer interns" from the two University based food co-ops affiliated with USA (another story in and of itself). It was the intention of this program to "educate" us as to the ways of a cooperative food store so that we could return to our respective food co-ops in the fall with a wealth of new and hopefully useful information and know how. While we did, in fact, do just that we also all became quite intrigued and enamored with Community Foods itself as we all continued to work there long after our college days.

I must explain that at this time, USA (University Services Agency) was an "umbrella" 501c3 non-profit corporation for many kindred and disparate businesses and services throughout Santa Cruz at that time. While USA began some years earlier, specifically to allow business not affiliated with the University to operate at the University, Community Foods (then operating in theory as a Co-op) became connected with USA sometime in the early '70s.

By the late '70s, there had been a "revolution" within USA and it was "taken over" by the "workers" of the various affiliates. With a shared idealism tempered with some real world practicality and "workplace democracy," the affiliate representatives would meet at monthly "board meetings" to share stories, questions, and information about their respective businesses.

By this time, Community Foods was no longer a Co-op and had evolved into a "worker owned and run collective," at least that was how it was represented and operated. My introduction to work there was via the "sub list." I was told that you simply put your name and phone number on this list and waited until if/when a "regular worker" needed their shift covered, they would most likely give you a call to see if you could cover it, or sometimes notes were posted on the bulletin board with "available sub shifts" and you could sign up. In this way, you familiarized yourself with the store, jobs, and "collective members." Eventually, and periodically, "regular workers" would give up a shift (or shifts) and post them as "available" for anyone to "sign up" for, after which it was the responsibility of the remaining workers of that particular shift to make their decision as to who they would like to fill the available shift, permanently. Congratulations were in order at that point, as one was now a "regular worker" and "collective member."

By the end of my summer internship, I was a "regular worker" on Friday afternoon, Saturday afternoon, and all day Sunday. Weekend shifts were the least desirable, but as a full time student, they fit my schedule just fine! As a "worker owned and run collective" we (the workers) were responsible for ALL ASPECTS of running and maintaining the store, I say "store" rather than "business" because at that time I'm not so sure we believed nor quite understood that it was a "business." Nonetheless, we "the workers" took responsibility for everything, although some workers assumed more responsibility than others—sometimes by design, sometimes by default. Although I can not recall exactly, In those days, we had probably somewhere between fifteen to twenty "collective members" and were grossing somewhere in the mid-to-high six figures, making us, far and away, the largest "affiliate" in USA, both in terms of workers and dollars.

We operated by "consensus," by that we meant that when an item was presented for discussion and/or decision at one of our meetings, it required the support ("consent" or at least no objection) from all "regular workers" in attendance. We had regular bi-weekly meetings, with posted agendas that anyone could add to throughout the week. Each meeting was chaired by a volunteer from the "collective." Topics of conversation might range from: day end clean-up procedures to new product considerations to wages & benefits-truly all aspects of running the store.

Now I imagine that there are still some out there that remember the building we rented on Commercial Way. To describe it as "funky" would be, even then, quite generous, but it was small and cheap! We knew that on a daily basis we could not stock the store with sufficient inventory to survive the day's demand, and as each day wore on it became a losing battle of attrition with the workers struggling to make it through the day without falling too far behind, eventually to be replenished each morning in order to just do it again, and again, and again.

One morning, just before opening, as we frantically

struggled to complete stocking, one of us actually fell through the floor (luckily it was only knee deep), yes it was that funky (decrepit). Quickly, with only minutes to spare before the opening onslaught, we nailed a board over the hole in the floor and proceeded to open on time. Just watch your step. But clearly, it was time to begin our search for a new location. To that end, one of our collective decisions was to keep our wages as low as possible (essentially at minimum wage) in order to build a moving fund for that eventual day.

I was affiliated with USA (University Services Agency), which provided a clearer legal status and a limit of any personal liabilities and business taxes. But over the years affiliation with USA had come to be seen as some sort of alternative socio-economic model for worker ownership and workplace democracy. "Affiliates" contributed an "affiliate fee" (loosely based on a percentage of their operations and in lieu of actual income taxes) to fund the staffing and overhead of "corporate" USA. As I said before, Community Foods was far and away the largest of these "affiliates" and as such, had the largest "affiliate fee." During these years (into the early '80s) the Community Foods Collective had few issues with this, although support for USA ranged from mild hostility, to benign neglect, to moderate support. However, this all came to an abrupt turnabout one year when the IRS audited USA and determined that while they may be a 501c3 nonprofit corporation, there were nonetheless several "for-profit" businesses (of which Community Foods was one) as a part of USA and they would therefore and in the future be subjected to "unrelated business income taxes" on the "profits" made by the "for- profit" businesses. For Community Foods, this meant in addition to paying our monthly affiliate fee (which we had largely viewed as our alternative to taxes) we now also had to pay real taxes!

To say the least, this did not go over too well with the Community Foods Collective, and the support for USA definitely shifted to a feeling that it was now time for us to "disaffiliate" from USA, incorporate for ourselves, and take responsibility for our legal status and taxes.

Moving the store and disaffiliating from USA put us in the midst of two major initiatives at once, but which would come to a head first? Nobody knew, so, a handful of us, working as representatives for the larger collective, pursued both, with the understanding that whichever reached a tipping point first would become the priority with the remaining project taking a back seat.

What came first was a new location at 2724 Soquel Ave, so we put all of our collective resources (energy, attention, and dollars) into remodeling the building, buying and building equipment and moving in. By the early '80s we were located in a newly refurbished building with approximately 2400+sf (square feet) of retail and 2400+sf of warehousing. The Way of Life, Indian Summer Juice Bar, and Santa Cruz Trucking also joined us in the move; however, their stories and relationships with Community Foods are other stories in and of themselves.

Throughout the '80s, Community Foods perhaps embodied the earliest definition of "too big to fail" as we were soon grossing over $2 million a year in our new retail space. It was often joked that we could stock the store over night, open the doors in the morning and just leave a coin box on the counter for shoppers to pay into, rinse and repeat. It seemed that our volume was so great that it often masked our inability to navigate our collective cumbersomeness and run an efficient business.

By the mid '80s, we were running pretty comfortably, at least from a cash flow perspective, and thought it was about time to circle back to USA and "disaffiliate." What had begun with a simple handshake among 1972 Santa Cruz idealists was not going to dissolve so easily. Remember how I said we were the largest affiliate with the largest affiliate fee? Remember how I said we decided to put all our collective resources (including dollars) into the move? Well, when we went to the USA board (which was made up of representatives of the various businesses and services), they were quick to see our proposed "disaffiliation" as the loss of their cash cow. While it was the position of the workers at Community Foods that the business was built as a result of their skills, energy, and efforts, and as we had contributed mightily to USA over the years, it was our right and their responsibility to support us in our independence. But that was not how USA came to see it and what resulted was a long acrimonious debate and fight, which in the end cost the workers of Community Foods $100,000 to buy their way out of USA!

By the mid '80s we successfully incorporated as Community Foods of Santa Cruz, Inc., and we did eventually complete payments to USA for our freedom. We were now truly a worker owned and run business! But where and how that goes into the '90s is a story for someone else to tell as I left Community Foods by 1989.

Mary Young and Allen Bernklau memories as dictated to Alayne Meeks

Community Foods now found itself thriving at the 2724 Soquel Ave location. Times were good. People could work for six months and then be voted, or not voted, into the workers' collective. Allen was voted in by 1984; Mary was already a member by then. There were renovations made and new bins purchased with the old bins given to General Feed and Seed where they are still in use today. Many a gourmet food show was attended with great anticipation of finding the right ingredients to make it to our shelves. We spent many hard hours planning advertising campaigns while spending endless hours negotiating for the best deals for our customers' benefit. We attended out of town Natural Foods Expo West and the San Francisco Gourmet Food shows. We were leaders in finding new products to enhance our shelves, and others followed suit.

Community Foods was a big cheese, yes, we bought enough cheese to be able to sell to others. We had cheese cutting shifts in our cheese room, we bottled our maple syrup that came from Vermont, we found deals on halvah, a sweet sesame treat, that we cut and packed in-house, we supplied bulk oils, vinegar, and soy sauce with a system on tap. Honey and molasses were sold in bulk and people would bring their own jars and fill them. Way of Life was in a separate building that adjoined the parking lot, Indian Summer Juice Bar, and the Flower Stand were also part of this grouping of businesses, but by then the trucking company had moved on.

Community Foods was also a conduit or diving board for many business success stories in Santa Cruz. Beckmann's Bread bought flour through Community Foods, and we bought his bread. Richard Alfaro started buying flour and ingredients through Community Foods then sold us his bread. Rebecca's Mighty Muffins bought ingredients for her muffins and sold them at Community Foods. These business interactions were always win-win situations. So many small businesses started buying their basic ingredients through Community Foods that eventually we connected them directly to the suppliers. Community Foods was a springboard to help businesses to move forward, just as the Co-op had done so many years before.

Many who had that co-op experience moved on to become masters of their own lives. Some started their own businesses that became hugely successful. We had one former member who became a civil rights attorney. We had bankers, musicians, accountants, and farmers who shared their talents or sold their products and became an intricate part of a much larger picture. Drew and Myra sold baby lettuce to Community Foods that they cleaned and dried in a wringer washing machine in their living room, and they went on to become Natural Selection, one of the biggest companies in the nation. Jeff Larkey was a grower with the Surf Monkey label, but he also started Route 1 Farms on Ocean St Extension and became a nationally recognized label. Some members of the produce department went on to pioneer new successful businesses that promoted organics on a local and national level. Coke farms, Vermont Farms maple syrup, Sciabica olive oil, Glaum eggs, Walls Honey Farm-we sourced so many local items in our search for clean and healthy food items. And Community Foods supported local artists who created advertising for the Sentinel, Good Times, Comic News, radio, and television. The store not only helped the community but the lives of many including workers, suppliers, and customers.

Community Foods continued to discuss, as is the workers' collective way, which items should be sold in the store, and in what direction the store should be headed. A beloved forklift, an Apple computer, and cash registers were added, and more people hired to do all the work. Each person had a specialty such as ordering fresh foods, ordering bulk items, bookkeeping, etc. But at some point the business became top heavy with workers, and it was clear too much money was going out. There were also expenses to maintain the store, periodically updating storage bins or walk-in refrigeration systems. The voting mechanism to allow workers into the collective was felt by some to be political or too personal, although the attempt was always made to ensure a good fit for the business, and those bulk sacks of food were not easy for anyone to lift. By the late '80s there may have been twenty-five to thirty collective workers, and the discussion was brought up that too many were working for the size of the existing business. Some quit, some took unemployment, so some returned and some did not, and this helped for a time. Even if you'd been a member in the past, if you applied for new member status it needed approval again.

Finally, by the early '90s, with ten to twelve members left, the financial situation became a problem again as there were losses from many sources. Some took advantage of the trusting nature of the business. There were even some successful robberies that damaged Community Foods economic situation, and the meetings became more contentious as the needs of the business came up against the will and the financial resources of the workers. Many times the workers couldn't agree on what to buy to move the business into more competitiveness with other natural foods stores. Sometimes topics were just not addressed as they became too emotional, but also with no decisions being made, no forward movement was made for the store. Then the discussion that a larger store was needed became a reality. The reality of capital improvements was ever present, as was the need for a larger space, but which way to go.

There were now only four financially viable workers able to take on a loan for improvements or a larger store. New hires were only interested in having a job, not in taking on the financial and emotional responsibilities of the collective. There was even a lawsuit filed against Community Foods over hiring practices. The lawsuit used Community Foods to bring up issues in the California Supreme Court, so the suit had never really been about the collective and they were exonerated but not before there were legal fees as well as emotional debt. Another difficulty was a buying club that used Community Foods' parking lot to sell goods directly to customers, thus reducing store purchases, and this buying club didn't seem to understand the damage it was doing. Finally there was another issue that loomed for Community Foods: A new business, Whole Foods, was building a location at the corner of 17th Ave and Soquel Ave, only 2 blocks away, and Whole Foods had a reputation for being very competitive. Suddenly the store and its workers were being bombarded from many sides. There was even a potential buyer who almost took over the business but withdrew at the possible reality of being a Whole Foods competitor. The future seemed to be clear that without heavy investments, and the fact that there was some internal turmoil between workers, the store should not continue. Interestingly, Whole Foods later sold to Staples, which is still at that location, and it took another ten years or more before Whole Foods came to Santa Cruz County.

As was a Co-op ethic, Community Foods thought of the community that had supported them through all these years, and while they could have chosen to just close the doors, cash in any profits and share them amongst themselves, they didn't. Community Foods did not want to hurt customers or vendors, so they sold things off slowly, stopped buying too many perishables or slow moving items, sold their food bins, cold storage refrigerators, hand trucks, anything that kept the store financially viable and paid all their bills while still bringing some bulk items to its customers at good prices. At this point collective workers were not getting paid, but hourly workers were. The Co-op workers did it for the love of the business, their customers, their vendors, and the ethic that they were part of a wonderful history and community and they would go out of business as respectful of everyone as possible. In 1994 it was time for the store to come to an end.

The last day saw India Joze working his wok magic with the leftovers in the store to feed those who had come to party and to say good bye to a local institution that had served people for almost twenty-five years. Vendors were invited, customers, anyone who'd been part of the community was welcome. Music was played, tears were shed, good food shared, and the doors were finally closed.

Final Thoughts by Alayne

In reading this and remembering the meetings, all the discussions, it seems that the best part of working with others was also the worst part. Too many differing ideas and the strong opinions of food oriented folks often left hurt feelings, but decisions had to be made if the business was to move forward. Eventually it seems that the cumbersome nature of trying to please everyone caught up with Community Foods and the noble attempt to run a business with as many as twenty-five differing opinions on how to do that aided in ending it. From the times of eating watermelons and having meetings in the back parking lot on North Pacific to the meetings Mary hosted at her house, the outcome was the same. You can't please everyone, but the need to make decisions has to happen for the successful life of a business. But when it came time to end, it ended well because the values instilled in its founding were carried throughout the business years even through its highs and lows. And the need for organic and local food was established early on by all the incarnations of this business, and that's a business model that continues to this day and that all members, workers,

vendors, and customers of the Co-op.
  Community Foods should be proud.

*Meeting of the Oral History Project at Bruce Damer's House 2012 (1)
From left to right (unknown), Glen Howard, T. Mike, Frank Forman, Ed
Penniman Nick Herbert, Bruce Damer (doorway), unknown on camera
(The white haired lady and the cameraman were from a Dutch-style PBS
station filming a documentary)*

*Estelle Fine, Bruce Damer, Ralph Abraham, Kate Bowland, Alex "Lex-
"van Zyll, unknown*

HOMESTEADING IN SANTA CRUZ
By F. John LaBarba

I know that a frog is an amphibian and a lizard is a reptile. But if it were possible to mix the two, you'd come close to what we saw slinking from behind the desk of T. Lester Burns, the day that we visited his office. We were to meet with him to discuss the details of us buying the property we were presently renting for $80.00 a month since September of 1973. I can't really say what kind of man T. Lester was; only that we were young, and he scared the shit out of us. He had been a Santa Cruz judge, but in his later years, had gone back to private practice. His eyes were beady and calculating, and while they shifted from left to right, there was always some premeditation before he would speak. His puffy checks were laced with the late stages of rosacea. This, combined with the deep wrinkles that pierced his face gave him the look of an old toad. "Ten Thousand dollars is not much money for a piece of property, " the toad chirped. Then he searched our faces for a response. I guess he could see the honesty in who we were, and that the whole property thing was new to us. He didn't mention it again, and ultimately the deal went through.

Lester was the attorney representing Mr. & Mrs. Harrison, who were now residing in New Mexico. His office was on the second floor of the Wells Fargo building, located at 74 River St. The structure built in the late 1960's, exemplified a time in the nation when the demolition of the "old and outdated" was extremely popular, and quickly being replaced by the "new." It seemed to be a feverish craze that was in the air at that time. Modern and new was good, and old seemed to be nothing but bad, ugly, and unwanted. Under the influence of urban renewal, or just being " modern" old wooden structures from the Victorian era were being replaced with cast cantilevered concrete and glass structures.   The Wells Fargo building being a prime example of one and replaced part of what had once been the area of the former Chinatown in Santa Cruz, an enclave of old Victorian and lesser buildings, residing next to the San Lorenzo River. A Buddhist temple finished up the grouping of the distressed wood, peeling paint, and partially rotted structures.

I don't think the city fathers missed any of the old Chinatown. A retired Santa Cruz County Sheriff, Al Bachtel, had once told me a story of how he had to close down the Chinese Fan Tan (Gambling) house located next to the river on Front street. The site of the former Longs Drugs, now CVS. Apparently one of the offspring from a prominent local family had lost a bundle gambling there. Don't remember if if was the Leask's, the Haber's or who it was. Consequently, the family was hell bent on closing down the place. The local Santa Cruz Police would not touch it, so they subcontracted the task to the sheriff's department, which at the time only had 9 deputies.

Beth Ann had spoken to Mrs. Harrison in New Mexico by mail and agreed on the sum of $10,000.00. We had been renting the property for over two years. We first found the place back in August of 1973, through our friend Diane. Prior to that, we had been living out of our trucks. I came with a 1960 Ford F-100 pick up, with an aluminum cab hight shell on the back. Beth Ann had a 1956 Chevy step side Apache pick up. With the help of another Los Angeles Artist, Dennis Handy, we created an"Over the cab", aged wood, rustic manifestation of the era. Beth Ann commonly referred to it as her Gypsy Wagon. Most the summer of '73 we would park at night against the tree line in a large field in Felton located on

Highway Nine, in-between the Quick Stop market, and what was once a pluming shop. Now it's a discount carpet place, the former field is now filled up with several buildings. During our entire stay there, no one ever said a word to us. Neither land owner or sherif.

The house was in such bad shape when we arrived that we spent several months cleaning it up, connecting utilities, and sleeping in our campers. Not knowing who the owners were, we just squatted there.

One day a couple showed up very angry, wanting to know why we were there. They later came back with the owners brother, a guy name Bob Agnew. He saw me, carpenter pencil in hand, replacing the bath room sub floor with new lumber, as the old had rotted out. After checking things out, Bob said to us, " I'm not going to decide this, you need to call my sister in New Mexico, and work things out with her, here's the number.

The mountain cabin, located on a little less the half acre, included an old Redwood septic tank, as was common in the Santa Cruz Mountains back then. There were no proper studs in the walls. The single story walls were built from 1" by 12" redwood planks, running from floor to ceiling. The only 2" by 4' framing was at the intersection of the floor to the walls and the same condition at the ceiling, with a little framing around the door and window openings.

The building had grown from a series of gabled roof structures. A flat roof covered with red colored rolled sheet roofing connected them all together. This area of the roof would become very familiar to me, as frequent visits with a can of wet patch roof cement and a putty knife, were to teach me at a young age the disadvantages of having a flat roof over your head. The floors were either unfinished Douglas fir boards, or covered with old marbleized linoleum flooring.

Bikers had been living in the house and abandoned it months before we found the place. The water line, from what we would later learn was a feeble example of a water well, had been disconnected. The main wall in the kitchen was white washed redwood planking and had become some kind of bulletin board for the previous occupants. A used Tampax hung from its string on a nail, along with various names and profanities that adorned the wall there. The inscription of " Subway Sam was here "was emblazed somewhere in the middle of it all. Looking back I guess this was not all that strange for the era. In less then ten years previous, the Summer of Love, Woodstock, and the film Easy rider had all occurred. So hippies and bikers alike, were occupying old farmhouses, or anything else they could find in the country. The term "back to the land" seemed to be everyone's mantra, and we were no exception to the movement. Finding a piece of land, and building you own house was one of the goals. Growing your own food, and being self-sufficient was a way of freeing yourself from the "establishment", and is something I still long for today.

After we closed the deal with the Harrison's and bought the property on Redwood Drive, Beth Ann got the money from her deaf father, Bernie, who was a typesetter for a newspaper in Cincinnati, Ohio. I won't get into the details about her father, but he had been divorced from Beth's mother since she was 5 years old. Bernie whore scars on the right side of his face, along with sporting a glass eye. Rumor has it the he was peeing in an alley while taking advantage of the view into the bathroom of the adjacent house. Whether he was actually seeing some one in the nude was never ascertained, but the occupant responded with a shotgun blast full of rock salt, sending him to the hospital. The eye was lost as a result.

When living in the country, the basic things that you have

taken for granted while living in the city abruptly become your responsibility. Like water and sewage treatment. After living in the front house for two years, we moved to the rear little cabin, and rented it to Sally, a woman recently separated from her husband, and her daughter Becky. Becky went to school with our daughter Kim, which is how we established the relationship.

All was well, or at least we thought it is was. We were trying our hand at being landlords, and with my part time carpentry jobs, we were managing to pay our bills. It wasn't long after we rented the house that the wet spot appeared on the bank below the corner of the house, and about four feet above the road. Every day the spot became larger until finally a stream of egg smelling effluent started seeping from the center of the spot, ultimately running down onto Redwood drive. This whole thing had really puzzled us, as it was only a month before that we had dug up the old wooden septic tank, and had Comstock Service suck it out. "The Comstock Load" was printed in quotes on the sides of Mr. Comstock's old tan 1960 Ford, cab over engine truck. The tank mounted on back of the truck, along with the hydraulic pump, showed the signs of the many years of service pumping and discharging the contents from countless septic tanks around the county.

If you can imagine W. C. Fields zipped up in a jump suit, then you were looking at Mr. Comstock. He even sounded a little like Fields. His sidekick, Chuck, a skinny beanpole type, operated the grease caked leavers of the hydraulic pump located at the back end of the tank. Comstock stirred the foul contents inside the Redwood box using a 9-foot long wooden handled spoon like tool. The sucker hose lunging and gasping as it was pulled in and out of the thick caustic soup. Occasionally the hose would clog up, chocking on a thick chunk of the stuff. Every time the line clogged, smoke would start to belch from the old hydraulic pump and Comstock would yell "Hey Chuck! Chuck! Shut it down, Chuck!"

We thought the job was finished. But now we had a foul smelling stream running down Redwood Road.

My friend Geo and I went down to the county building and asked the environmental health department if there were any records concerning the property. To our surprise the clerk handed us a copy of a crudely drawn plan of the front yard showing the placement of the leach line with dimensions. As crude as the drawing was, we found the dimensions to be accurate. We started digging at the south end of the line furthest from the tank. Within a foot or so of soil we hit the tarpaper membrane protecting the drain field. After another few inches of digging through the ¾" drain rock, we saw the top of the pipe.

It was then known as "Orange-burg Pipe," made of ground cellulose (wood) fibers that were bound together with a special water resistant adhesive, and impregnated with liquefied coal black tar pitch. This was an innovation in the industry, and replaced the heavier and more expensive steel and terra cotta pipes in sewer application. During the post war years of 1948 and on, the building boom brought production of the pipe to its zenith. The largest producer was located in Orange-burg, New York, hence the name. Later, with the invention of PVC pipe in the 1960's, the production of Orange-burg pipe stopped in 1972, being replaced by the cheaper, stronger, and lighter competitor.

Another characteristic of the strange pipe was that it started to deform when buried and not compacted just right. In fact, most of the Orange-burg pipe that I've exhumed in my career seemed to suffer from this affliction, making it more oval in shape, then round. With the walls of the pipe being relatively soft, we were able to bust through it using a hammer. To our surprise, what we witnessed inside the pipe was a dry, clean inner lining, only being occasionally interrupted by very small white colored plant roots. From there we dug just above the tarpaper membrane, following the line for 40 feet or so. According to the drawing, the leach line ended within another ten or more feet from where we had stopped digging our shallow trench. We figured it was another place that we should inspect, and busted through the top section of the asphalt-based product. Here again, the same condition revealed itself.

Earlier that day we had dropped by the local tool rental place, and rented a power actuated drain cleaning snake. Gail, the owner, may have had a thing for me at that time, as she always seemed to reveal it slightly in something she would say, and or certain look in her eye as we would complete our rental transaction. The Snake, as commonly referred, would prepare us for the unknown conditions that we would surly encounter. . At that point it was time to initiate the tool we had rented, so up the line toward the septic tank we drove our oscillating probe. Upon reaching the tank we hit the solid wall of Redwood and started to extract our much appreciated mechanical helper. A popping sound came from the inside of the pipe as I pulled the end of the snake out. Attached to the spring shaped end was a full sized Wonder Bread bag, whose contents we would latter find out were used sanitary napkins.

Following the popping sound came a deep guttural noise from within the composite conduit. It was loud enough to capture our attention, causing us to look down and then jump back. What started to emerge from the broken end of the pipe was no less that a 4 inch diameter, black turd whose extruded mass revealed itself like toothpaste squeezed from it's tube. Ling straight up, it wavered like a black cobra ready to attack. The anomaly stood there momentarily, then fell over, breaking up into random sections. The salubrious mass lay there undulating as if it had a life of it's own. The parade of sewage accelerated, only to be followed by yet another uncorking, as a black liquid came rushing out from the pipe. What saved us that day from the black scourge was the stream, which followed the low point of our ditch creating a 40-foot long rushing unnatural creek that disappeared at the end of our ditch down the first hole we made in the pipe.

Later that day, after patching the pipe and membrane, covering up the ditch, and hosing every thing down, we set out to exhume our septic tank again. Upon lifting the Redwood 2" by 8" tongue and grooved boards that made up the top of the tank, the whole incident became clear to us. The baffle in the tank was made up of 1" by 6" boards, and the top one had worked its way loose. This allowed anything floating in the first compartment to float it's way over to the second chamber. The bread bag must have floated over and lodged itself somewhere along the discharge end of the pipe. The dam this created stopped any effluent from reaching our leach field, emerging in the soil near the road. We never asked Sally or her daughter who flushed the bag, and to this day cant figure out how they ever got it to go down the toilet.

Our friend, "Bruce the poet", was a very talented at what he did, and would never miss a chance to remind you of this. He was one of the few people to gain the accolade of being 86ed from both the old Catalyst located on Front Street, and the later version built on Pacific Ave. I don't know if it was because of his knack for getting in your face to press whatever issue he felt was important at the moment, or his standing on tables with his friend Barney, tearing up dollar bills to prove that money didn't matter to him. I think he got the idea from his frequent reading of Rambo.

Bruce's normal scenario was to stay with friends, or people he would meet, eat, drink and abuse as long as he could be tolerated. Then after being kicked out, he would find his way to your doorstep, drunk, marooned, and begging for a place to stay, only to start the cycle over again. We were one of the few people that maintained a relationship with Bruce for over 35 years, before finally throwing in the towel. I think your tolerance for putting up with abusive behavior starts to run thin, as you get older.

He did have his redeeming qualities though. Bruce was capable of being a nice, sensitive, intelligent person, and a hard worker, when it came to physical tasks. We did have many pleasant times together while working and relaxing. There will always be a warm place in our hearts for him, and many fond memories of the good times that we did share together. At a recent memorial for a close friend and neighbor of 39 years, Bruce read a poem paying tribute to the man's life. With all the alcoholism, and crap that has gone on in his life, Bruce hasn't lost his touch for putting poetry to paper.

When not engulfed in the throngs of an alcoholic bender, he would bury himself into Christianity. It is probably the one thing that has kept him alive. Bruce was constantly meeting and using people. Many of his "friends" at that time, would cross the street in order to avoid him. If he was standing in front of the old Cooper House, they'd wait until he was gone before approaching the place. But still he'd manage to find people to hang out with. It was one of these interactions that would ultimately bring Rambling Jack Elliot to our humble, unfinished cabin one evening.

It was after we had bought the property on Redwood drive, and we were living in a small cabin behind the main house. We had rented out the main house to help pay our debts. John, a teacher at Cabrillo College, and Dora a hippy violinist, with her little son, Kuwana, rented the main house from us. It was our second attempt at being a landlord there, and turned out to be just as unfruitful as our first attempt with Sally.

Bruce, the poet had been by our place earlier in the week, and was with a fellow who said he was a friend to Jack Elliot. Bruce seemed determined to have us meet Jack, I think he may have even used our encounter with Dylan to entice him, I don't really know. One evening we decided to have a small party, and I started an open fire in front of our tiny cabin. The fire was contained by a square stack of used bricks, and an old refrigerator shelf that doubled as a barbecue grate. Red Snapper sizzled on the grill.

We had invited a few folks, Bruce the poet, being invited of course. My boss, also named Bruce, was Bruce Gambee. He and his wife Sandra had arrived, our close friend Geo, with beer bottle in hand was there, and a few others that I can't seem to remember. Before long, we had consumed the fish, and drank ourselves into a jolly state. Upon the 2"x 8" unfinished wood floor of our cabin, I sat in an old style, spring loaded office chair, next to an old pine farm table our friend Steven had given us. Geo, sitting across from me at the table, leaned into his chair taking in the night's energy. We had found the office chair along with a the better part of a blue steel child's petal toy that was in the shape of a 1950's style rocket ship. Thoughts of Flash Gorden passed through my mind as I pulled it from a pile of junk at the "AS IS" portion of the Goodwill collection yard that was located just off Encinal Street in Santa Cruz.

The pair of doors on our shack were open, so from my vantage point I could see all our friends sitting fireside, and hear what was going on. From the dark emerged Bruce, his new made friend, and Jack Elliot. After a brief introduction,

Jack came in and sat at the table with my friend Geo and I. We had just opened a half pint on I W Harper, and I was quick to offer it to our new guest. He reciprocated, and the bottle went around between the three of us until it was empty.

Outside in the fire light, Bruce the poet started to recite, "The fox sniffs the edges of the woodlands," he went on, using his poet like staccato phrasing, and making hand gestures to enunciate his spoken words. Upon finishing, we all clapped acknowledging Bruce's artistry. After several more, Beth Ann grabbed her guitar and started to sing. I was 24 years old, and happy to be alive. My wife's voice rang out into the night enhancing the good feelings we all shared. Jack leaned over towards me and made a hand jester toward my boss Bruce Gambee, who was sitting outside.

Bruce Gambee was an unusual looking man. He combed his hair straight back, and used a type of butch wax to keep it that way. To me it was a personification of photos I had seen of men in the 1920's and 30's.

Standing over six foot tall, he would walk with a stature of confidence, spouting off his observations, and nodding his head while presenting his point of view. He was not a lot older that us, but it felt like he was due to his look and mannerisms. He had a space between his two front teeth, button type checks, and always wore long sleeve shirts. He continued to roll up the cuffs of his jeans that were to long, something I hadn't seen since the 1950's. Later on I came to realize that my former boss bore a striking resemblance to Doc Ricketts, of Steinbeck's fame. It was a strange set of circumstance that Bruce was the first person to tell me to read Tortilla Flat, and Cannery Row.

When he spoke, his voice was high-pitched, winy, and could be raised a few octaves when fueled with excitement. While talking he'd use terms like, "How goes the war," or

"That's better than a sharp stick in the eye." He told us about the days when he worked with a framing crew. A grazing blow with the hammer sent a 16-penny nail straight into his eye. He pulled the nail out but had to keep a finger on it while traveling to the hospital to keep the inner fluid from leaking out. He had participated in and won several championships in duet roller skating in the Monterey Bay area. Skating in pairs, similar to ice skating routines. I was told that's what started his butch wax hair treatment as a means of keeping the hair in place while performing his act.

Bruce had worked in construction since he was a boy. An old time contractor in Carmel Valley, Hal Porter, had taken him under his wing, and through Hal, Bruce had become accomplished builder in his own right. We looked up to him, and learned a lot from him, but there were times he treated us badly, down right dysfunctional for that matter. He would delegate a task to one or more of us, knowing that we were unsure how to execute it. Then when we would screw up, he would verbally brow beat us, and enjoy himself while doing so. This would happen on a regular basis. He would also create a pecking order among us when the crews where larger, sending our friend Steven off crying at least once that I can remember. Years later when I was on my own, I would call Bruce for advice, as I still respected him, but it would be several years before I got rid of the chip on my shoulder his ridicule had put there.

The night of our party Bruce Gambee wore a dark blue windbreaker, with the name of his jeep club silk screened on the back. Bruce's over all look gave Rambling Jack the creeps, and he asked me if Bruce was a narc.

I assured Jack that he was my boss and not a cop. Later that evening we managed to get of the subject of land ownership. Jack was getting ready to buy a piece of land in Santa Cruz, I think off Old San Jose Road, but I'm not sure.

I don't know if that was Jack's first piece of property, but he was quite troubled at the thought of owning land. "It's really no big deal," I told him. "No big deal at all," Here I was just a kid, comforting a man who was not only older than me, but much more worldly as well. It felt awkward, but I did the best I could to console him. "You just own it and deal with it, that's all, " I said with conviction.

John & Beth Ann LaBarba, Wedding Pictures

Jack looked over at me and I wasn't sure if what I had said had sunk in. That was the end of the conversation on land though, and we never went back to it. The music went on and the night ended peacefully, but I can't remember when Jack, Bruce the poet, my boss, or anyone else left. The next morning I woke up to find Geo on the floor in the corner by where we kept our shoes, in his sleeping bag sawing logs. The fire had long since gone out, and Rambling Jack's visit was already just a memory.

John and Beth Ann's Wedding Party Round Dance at their home

THE PERFORMING YEARS IN SANTA CRUZ
by Beth Ann and John Labarba

We took everything we had, which was not much, and our dreams, and moved to Santa Cruz in 1973. That summer we camped a lot in Felton, and on Empire grade. I worked at the Shire in Ben Lomond, and John got a job making Adobe bricks in Boulder Creek. He'd come home to the Shire, and shower off with the hose outside. I'd serve food, and sing in the early evening. Later I got a gig at the Felton Guild every Friday night. I was 26 years old. That was 50 years ago.

John finished out in Cabrillo college, and then went on to UCSC, and was an art major. John worked at the colleges, and making adobe bricks, or handy man work for all of our neighbors. We got to be a Camp Joy for the Barn raising too. I was lucky enough to get some studio work at Tiki Studios in San Jose through Brandy Bento who later would be Micheal McDonald's girlfriend, and get him the gig with the Doobie's in LA. Brandy got me the gig doing the backup singing on Chuck McCabe's Pensacola Flash album. And some singles.

I have been always lucky to stumble into some kind of group of people doing some kind of art project, music, or performance. When we first got to Santa Cruz we were squatting at an abandoned house a friend (Diane Marvin) told us about. Sleeping in our campers just out side of town. We burned, and hauled trash, and got the water, and power hooked up. Put in a garden. The kids were in school. Then we searched for the owners. Eventually renting, and then buying the house with help form my family. We had a 3rd child in 1975. Five years later selling to buy across the road 12 acres with a shack, and a spring.

We were young. I first met Climbing Sun, and David Thierman at the Good Fruit Company on Front street, and started playing there. In 1979 pregnant with my 4th child at 32   I stumbled into a Kathak Class with Gita Jan. Sign being my first language having deaf parents, and seeing all of the hand gestures of Kathak, I just started to cry. I began studying with her for the next year, and a half, and off, and on through the years. When my last baby was about 6 months old my dear friend Diane Marvin came by to tell me about the African dance classes in town with Marian Oliker, and about the Calamari Festival. She said I should write a song for the festival. So I did. Inspired by David Bowie's Golden Years song...

"I finally tried it
tried Calamari
Not Matahari
A Calamari
It's so Squidie
I eat, and eat, and eat Just like miss piggy..."

I started going to African classes, and that was it. I wrote a song for the festival. We put a band together with some back up dancers including Diane, and we performed it at the Art League. The next year I was the Queen " Oct-ti-Punk " with the Batteries backing me up with back up dancers. My daughter, and I won first prize for our costumes I made for the Carnival Festival at Joze's.

Joe Shultz, and Beth Regards were living in midtown in the back of a store, I think. Judy Slattem invited me to be in The Hit And Run Medicine Show group, and we did a lot of shows that season. After a year I was going to African dance 3 days a week. Eventually drumming for classes at UCSC, and substitute teaching the dance class myself at the Louden

Center. Soon making costumes, and performing in 3 different troupes—Hearts of Art, Rhythm Rites, Escolanova de Samba, and drumming too. I made costumes for Tao Chemical, Tao Rhythmical, and got to dance, and sing with them. But all along I took 3 semesters of modern dance at Cabrillo, and studied Iyengar Yoga with Ann Barros too.

I also was hanging out at Mt. Madonna doing the Ramayana. I also started a love affair with Flamenco in 1985. All of this with a husband becoming a contractor, and me raising 4 kids mind you…We were building a workshop studio first so we could be somewhere to sleep, and have a shop to build the house, Then we would tear down the old cabin, drilling a well, and living in a trailer part time, and then the studio with no bathroom or kitchen. We had to commute to the old kitchen for Breakfast, and dinners for 4 years. We were roughing it for sure. Reminds me of the song, "There was an old woman who swallowed a fly. I don't know why she swallowed the fly, perhaps she'll die…"

In 1987 I was invited by my Flamenco teacher Cristobal Mair to dance in El Amor Brujo at UCSC along with the Santa Cruz Ballet. By 1986 I met Emily Maine, and started studying Baratanatyam dance with her. She would be the most intensive teacher I ever met, an incredible human being so devoted to her art form, and a Theravata Buddhist who lived in Burma for a while. She was the second person I knew who studied Burmese Buddhism in Burma. She had all of us perform in the Ramayana one year opening the show.

Then, in 1987, after living in a studio for 4+ years while building our house, we had a dance studio: One World Music and Dance Studio. I offered it to all of my teachers for free, and new young people who wanted to teach in exchange for my classes. We never charged for the studio, and I would make ads and posters for the classes, workshops, performances, and trunk sales we produced. In 1991 we began a yearly 21 Praises of Tara workshop with Prema Dasara. We would also take her classes in Oddisi Dance and open the shows with the Tibetan Heart Sutra. We'd needed to invite a lama to do the blessing, so we spent a lot of time at the different Tibetan monasteries in Santa Cruz.

In 1995 I started playing contemporary music again solo, at home alone, inspired by the CD Largo. And in 1997 I did a workshop at D'ror's Rhythm Fusion with Layne Redmond, and Glen Valez. Emily's then husband Ron who was working with Cirque in Japan, called her from LA while she was in Santa Cuz working at Industrial Light and Magic, to tell her to take Suhail Caspar's drum class at Rhythm Fusion so we did. I got Hooked. I was collecting quite a few drums by then already from my African dance days. A Dij, here, a tambora there, and some accordions.

I started learning Arabic drumming, and that blended into even more forms of music, chanting, singing, and dance. We became very close to Sol Feldthouse's family because he was playing every Friday night for our Flamenco classes. It was incredible how many different teachers came through over the years. And there it was—ATS American Tribal Style Dance it had everything combined in it. HEAVEN!!! Colleena Shakti, Elizabeth Strong, Mira Betz, the beautiful talented Katarina Burda, Jess, and all of the teachers too many to mention. Dan Cantrell, Stellmara, Dervish dancers, Balkan players.

Then The Aza boys from Morocco moved into Santa Cruz, so I got to study with Mohamed and Fattah ,singing, playing banjo, and drumming. All the while doing Flamenco, tap, Bulkan singing, dancing, drumming, drum making, Cherokee/Tibetan, Chi Kung, Hawaiian, Indonesian, Roma, and Sufi meditations.

We built my mother a house next door, which became available because she had to go to a nursing home. We had divided it into 2 cottages, one for a for a caretaker. And now we were housing artists from Spain, Turkey, the Bay Area, and all over. Slowly it came to a close in 2014. Our youngest daughter moved into my mother's place in 2007, and they have had 3 babies since then. We are a tribe. It takes a village. My Hero, my mother, passed away in 2016. And now it's a whole new life. The Harvest...

I managed to buy Page Smith's table from his estate sale. It is lovingly kept in my dance studio today. I always imagine he and Paul Lee, maybe Jasper Rose, or Mary Holmes at the table. Maybe even Huey Newton. John and I got to go to Jasper's house a few times to hike and paint. I was so lucky to visit Mary Holme's beautiful place. UCSC, the farm, and the Chadwick Garden are the pillars of my heart's space. I am still close to Jane Madsen who invited me into her home in Felton in 1970. She still lives there today. The idea of all of those men and women fighting the good fight. Homeless Garden project. Mark Primack, saving the trees from the Tree Circus in Scotts Valley, and his incredible family.

We became very close to Fred Hunicutt and his wife at College Five. We have been forever changed by Ralph Abraham, Terrance McKenna, and Rupert Sheldrake in the Trilogues. Gone are the days of Mae Brussell. Gone are the days of Dr. Stan Monteith. These are the new intense days we are facing. Just seeing Ralph Abraham walking in and out of New Leaf Market, or at Omei in town.

I remember the first time I got to walk through the forest and Rhododendrun bushes to T. Mike Walkers Tipi at Cabrillo College. What a dream. And now to read his writing in the books! I am always so glad to see him through the Flamenco, and Renfare families. And here we are 2024

I have been so lucky to be able to read this series, and find out more about all of the movers, and shakers that made "Santa Cruz" the epicenter of mind that it is…I thank all of the ancestors, indigenous and otherwise, who kept this place. I send you all my deepest love, and appreciation.

I still remember going to a beach house in Santa Cruz hear a talk by Baba Hari Das. (Ralph Abraham was part of a large portion of the community who brought Hari Das Baba to town, where he opened Mt. Madonna School) My parents were deaf, and always used a pad and pencil to "speak", so I felt a weird connection with him right away. But what was it? Then the second time we saw him he was giving a talk in a house off of Ocean street. We were all seated on the floor, and Babaji was speaking to us with writing. Eventually he said he had a friend who would sing about God.

I had seen this guy sitting on the floor, a kind of a surfer looking guy, with a cute curly red headed girlfriend. He had big black shades on. I thought, "What is this heroin attic looking guy doing here?" He no longer had dreds, as he had in the photos of him in the book, but he was Bhagavan Das. He sang the most heavy, earthy, soulful gospel blues I'd ever heard. And s few days later there they were, Bhagavan Das, Ush and the baby on River Street, standing in front of the Good Fruit Company on North Pacific avenue.

I said ,"Hi, I'd really like to sing backup for you

He said, "I can't afford to pay anyone. "

I don't want money. "

The next thing I knew I was rehearsing with Ram Das, Kali Ray, Mercury Max, for a concert at the Santa Cruz Civic. I also got to preform in several Ramayana's with Babaji, and cast of dozens. Once I danced as a "Guha", and the next time I danced Baratanatyam with our teacher Emily Maine…I remember looking at Babaji the whole time dancing the opening of the show...Words can not describe what I experienced. Later I was able to sing with the choir and on tapes with everyone. I felt very blessed. Bhagavan Das would later witch the water well where we still live today. I would help them move from one place to another. He would borrow my gypsy wagon to sell things at the flea Market. One day up at Mount Madonna center, through the big window of the kitchen, I saw a group of people crowded around Babaji. He was busy writing to them all. I realized my parents had no choice, they were deaf. But Hari Das Baba took on Not Speaking by choice—although he did sing the Bajans with us! But Babaji could actually hear!

So thank you Babaji, and to everyone for keeping the flame going. I am so lucky to be able to read this series, and find out more about all of the movers and shakers that made "Santa Cruz" the epicenter of mind that it is. I thank all of the ancestors, indigenous and otherwise, who kept this place. I send you all my deepest love, and appreciation.

Beth Ann and her Gypsy Wagon mobile home, 1973

Beth Ann, Queen Oct-ti-Punk w/ Batteries, 1982

Beth and John Labarba 2024

IF THERE'S A POLITICAL CAMPAIGN, EXPECT TO SEE JOHN LAIRD

by Don Monkerud

In November 1983 it was time for a celebration. Not only had his council candidates won, but he would also become the next mayor. After a long, arduous campaign, he could relax at last. But not quite.

The following week, newspapers around the state and the nation carried a story about him being one of the first elected gay mayors in California. John Laird, the first openly gay person elected as mayor, would face what he calls a "media riot." His phone didn't stop ringing as reporters clamored for interviews. The Paul Harvey news covered his election. His story became an item on local and national TV news, and letters flooded in.

"I never intended this to happen," says John. "It wasn't deliberate, but I was happy to have the story out and be able to deal with it. I was comfortable with being gay, but my contract was with the people of Santa Cruz, a promise that I would be a good mayor."

Throughout the interviews, John focused on a bill in the California State Legislature, sponsored by Art Agnos (D) San Francisco, that would end discrimination in employment based on sexual orientation. Fully knowledgeable and experienced in local government, John had done everything he could to avoid bias because of his sexual orientation.

The matter of John's sexual orientation wasn't an issue in the election in Santa Cruz and only came up after Jack Foley, a reporter from the San Jose Mercury News, took John to lunch for an interview and asked if he was gay. John jokes that only 6,000 to 7,000 people in Santa Cruz knew. He had endorsements from gay and lesbian groups in the city but didn't see any other candidates calling a press conference to proclaim their sexual orientations. He saw no need to do so. The Phoenix, a weekly Santa Cruz newspaper, did run a front-page story wondering whether John would be a single-issue candidate focusing on gay issues. Still, John had too much experience in all areas of county government for the story to be taken seriously by the voters. The conservatives split over whether to make it an issue in the campaign and ended up ignoring it.

"The significant thing that came from the election wasn't about my career but the coalition that won," reflects John. "It brought neighborhoods, women's groups, labor, peace groups, gay and lesbian groups, students, affordable housing supporters and others together. Voters elected Mardi Wormhoudt and I to join Mike Rotkin in the city council, and for the first time, there was a non-conservative majority. That hasn't shifted in the years since."

Because John hadn't considered that his parents hadn't told their friends he was gay, his outing had unexpected personal consequences. His brother, also gay, called to say Wendy Tokuda was calling him an avowed homosexual on a Bay Area TV newscast. "It's like a funeral around here," his brother, the family comedian, hooted. "People are bringing casseroles." His parents already knew he was gay, and discussing his private life on TV brought surprising and uplifting results. One woman wrote thanking him. She had three gay sons, and John would make their lives easier. His mother received a letter from a friend saying she had always snickered when Harvey Milk, the gay San Francisco supervisor, came on TV. She knew the Lairds were a loving family and realized their private lives weren't anyone's business. She would never snicker at a gay again.

The immediate events leading up to John's election and nine years, from 1981 to 1990, on the city council grew out of his disappointment trying to work with the conservative-dominated council. In 1976, he became part of a blue ribbon city committee to review the city charter. Made up of former mayors and other experienced members, the committee took a year to draft the proposed changes. But the handwriting was on the wall, and change was in the air. The conservative majority that had held sway over city politics since the city's founding was on the way out, and they did everything they could to prevent the change. The council angered many in the community by ignoring the draft of proposed changes. John sat through city council meetings and knew he had the skills and knowledge to do a better job than they were doing. Except he was gay, and Harvey Milk, a gay San Francisco city council member, had just been killed, essentially for being gay. Could John ever hope to run for political office?

John was facing a choice and admitted it was difficult for him. He had worked in county government, in highly responsible, stressful jobs, for six years, first on a congressional district staff and then as an analyst for Santa Cruz County. In 1974, he began working directly for the chief administrator of county government, assigned to health and social service programs. This was the first time revenue-sharing grants were given. John administered the contracts for fifty non-profits, coordinating all procedure phases, from grant applications to board funding and reporting. He learned how county government worked—county procedures, budgets, and the financial details of Santa Cruz County. This period became an intense learning experience. Involvement in public policy requires working with different people to make things work. Issues need to be defined clearly. Good interpersonal relations are a must, and solid groundwork is necessary to bring people together. Joining a drop-in gay men's group that met on Monday nights in Louden Nelson Community Center boosted his self-confidence. He brought the skills he learned together in his public and personal life, which served him well when he ran for the city council.

"At first, only ten to twelve men showed up for the meeting, but the group quickly grew to seventy-five to ninety men," recalls John. "We would break up and talk in small groups and then meet as a full group; I developed self-confidence in those meetings. These were men in the community: doctors, bus drivers, lawyers, waiters, teachers, and a whole mix of people who, to this day, are still some of my best friends. We bonded. The group created a real turning point because it made us understand how much power we had when we all came together. We developed a comfort level because we could fall back on other men from every walk of life, and it was less risky to be openly gay and out there at the time."

The group was saddened and shocked when San Francisco city supervisor Dan White got a light sentence for gunning down Harvey Milk. John watched the news just before attending a gay group meeting, and he arrived to find some of the other men so shaken they couldn't talk about it. Others were so angry they piled into cars and drove to San Francisco to protest. The shooting occurred just at the time when John was wondering whether to enter politics himself. If such a high-profile supervisor could be gunned down, how could he establish a political life himself? If Harvey Milk couldn't make it, could anyone? It became a great personal dilemma.

"Harvey Milk's death followed on the heels of my political coalition work and my advocacy on public policy issues, water, transit, and other issues," John explains. "With his death, I realized I had to choose between being openly gay and comfortable in my life or never holding a high rank in government, whether by appointment or election."

John took a year off to travel to Mexico, Guatemala, and Bolivia and mulled over what he wanted to do with the rest of his life. He studied Spanish and wrestled with his dilemma. During the trip, he realized that if Harvey Milk's death and other's opposition to gays discouraged him, he was giving those who discriminated and hated control over his life. If they prevented him from running, they would be rewarded for excluding others from the political process.

"They didn't deserve to be rewarded," says John. "I came back to Santa Cruz feeling liberated. I was comfortable with myself and had support from an active gay community." At last, he reconciled his interest in politics with being gay.

Upon his return, John had barely settled into his job before a controversy rocked the community. Undercover police entrapped sixteen men in Capitola and arrested them for being gay. The Sentinel and the Pajaronian published their names and home addresses. The gay community was enraged, as were others. John and Jerry Solomon, a local therapist, visited the Capitola police chief to point out the outrageousness of the arrests.

"We had a two-hour appointment, and he talked for an hour and fifty-five minutes," John recalls. We couldn't get a word in edgewise."

Undaunted, John helped set up three-person teams, a resident of Capitola, a gay man or lesbian, and an attorney or business owner, to talk to Capitola city council members. One threw them out of his business; most refused to meet with them. Pushing on, the group planned to attend a Capitola city council meeting. Two-hundred-and-fifty people, including representatives from legal groups, the Gray Panthers, gay and lesbian activists, and other community groups, argued that gays shouldn't be entrapped or targeted by the police. The council agreed to seek training for the police and to stop the entrapment, although John points out that they later undermined their agreement. Looking around the room that night, John realized the power people held when they organized. He decided to try to focus on this power and, the following year, ran for Santa Cruz City Council.

His political blossoming became a long journey. John grew up in the working-class town of Vallejo on the Carquinez Straits, where his father was a teacher and principal in the small sugar-refining town of Crockett. The city had a diverse ethnic mix of African-American, Filipino-American, and working-class whites. He entered school in 1955 and graduated with the same group of kids in 1968. Out of a high school graduating class of three-hundred-and-fifty students, just fifteen continued on to a four-year college. He describes his high school experience as straight out of the movie Hairspray, where girls wore beehive hairdos, kids smoked in the bathrooms, and the fight for civil rights was in your front yard. Life was real and down-to-earth, which prepared John for everything in his later life.

John's parents met while attending the University of South Dakota. His father, the son of the head of the plumber's union local and a phone operator, was the first Laird in his family to go to college and also the first Laird in five generations to leave Danville, Illinois. On his mother's side, his grandparents moved from the Midwest to Cotati, where his grandfather maintained a small ranch on the Gravenstein Highway and managed a lumberyard. His grandmother was one of California's last grade school teachers without a college degree.

John's father, a high school principal, participated in

every community activity and coached a championship high school basketball team. Most of these activities included the family. John had two younger brothers and grew up playing baseball and basketball in the streets with other kids, attending Saturday afternoon cinema, and living a normal childhood.

Between his junior and senior years in high school, John entered a foreign studies program in Spain, living with an attorney's family. This life-changing experience made him question everything in his life, including wanderlust. Since then, he has traveled to 46 states and 50 countries; he travels yearly, exploring different cultures around the world.

John dated girls in high school and took a good friend, a Korean-Chinese American woman, who later became one of the first to visit Cuba with the Vencermos Brigade, to the prom. It was an interracial date, but he didn't consider it such then, for he grew up in a household dedicated to civil rights. His father wasn't outspoken—the only bumper sticker John recalls his father putting on the family car was in support of fair housing—but his father quit the local church when the congregation indicated they wouldn't accept a black minister. John fit in and got along with everyone.

"The only thing that set me apart from many other kids was that I was an avid reader," John explains. "Plus, I was always interested in current affairs. I kept a scrapbook on the Kennedy-Nixon campaign when I was ten. A senior in 1968, I spent six months working on Eugene McCarthy's campaign, my first active political campaign."

A serious student, John had the top G.P.A. among boys and enrolled at UCSC, which was in its fourth year. Nixon bombed Cambodia in 1969, and the peace movement was in full swing. John attended teach-ins and demonstrations in Berkeley, 20 miles away from Vallejo, and got involved in anti-war protests. In 1970, he went with 75 students to Washington, D.C., to lobby Congress against the war, his first experience with tear gas during a May Day demonstration. In 1970, he served as a Contra Costa County staff member on the Jerry Waldie congressional campaign, and in the summer of 1971, he went to Washington, D.C., as an intern for Pete McCloskey, who ran as a peace candidate against Nixon in the primaries.

"Tear gas was a real eye-opening experience," John said. "We spent two weeks lobbying legislators, the state department, anyone who would talk to us about the war. It led me to return to Washington the following year and work for an anti-war candidate. Politics were an integral part of college, and anti-war activity was at its heart."

The year 1972 was an active time for the anti-war movement at UCSC. In February, John organized a campus meeting for George McGovern, the peace candidate, that drew 80 students to help on the campaign. McGovern took over 90 percent of the campus vote, followed by Shirley Chisholm, another anti-war candidate from New York, and Hubert Humphrey in third place. His work for McGovern led to his becoming a delegate to the 1972 Democratic Convention in Miami Beach, Florida.

John recalls the spring of 1972 sit down on Highway One, although he missed being arrested because he was working at campus food services to pay his tuition. After the police arrested one hundred and seventy-five people, he arrived in time to join a march to the jail. He watched the Tactical Squad run down the street to protect the Bank of America when students marched on it, the memory of the burning bank in Santa Barbara still fresh in their minds. During "a strange moment," John recalls sitting as a city council member at a dinner honoring the retirement, after 25 years, of the police chief who presided over these arrests and enduring speakers referring to the event as the chief's "finest hour."

John realized he was gay during college. Although he dated women, he had no role models, and no one spoke about being gay. Slowly, he discovered that he was more attracted to men than women and credits the atmosphere in Santa Cruz with allowing people to discover their sexual orientation without angst-creating social pressure. For example, in 1975, Santa Cruz was the first county in the nation to ban discrimination of county employees based on sexual orientation. John's sexual orientation made no difference in the local political scene.

Active on the Inter College Board as one of two representatives from Stevenson College, John recalled the frustration of students without a real student government. The chancellor controlled students' decisions, which led to their becoming uproariously irreverent. They abolished the council. At every student council meeting, they passed a resolution demanding that the U.S. immediately withdraw from Vietnam. While a great comedy, UCSC also had a serious side; it forced him to think critically, write, and seriously apply himself to his studies. Additionally, he focused on studying politics.

His senior thesis, a study of the history of water development in California, examined environmental issues: where water was diverted, the effect of diversions on the San Jacquin River delta, social issues created by subsidized water, the support of large agri-business as opposed to family farms, and other financial and political issues. The thesis weighed in at 160 pages.

"The thesis surprised me," John admits. "I had no idea doing a thesis on that topic would change the rest of my life. I was always an enviro, and a coastie – and that central valley agriculture interests and urban southern California drove water policy. I never thought I would be the cabinet secretary responsible for state water supply."

After graduation, John took a position with Congressman Jerry Waldie, when he became a candidate for governor, and whom he had interviewed for his senior thesis. John brought environmental expertise to the staff because Waldie was one of the few candidates speaking out on land ownership patterns in agriculture and environmental degradation caused by diverting water from the San Jacquin Delta. This experience later helped John when he worked on the Joint Powers Agreement, a region-wide study of land use and water for Santa Cruz County.

After Waldie lost his bid for governor, John took a job on a day's notice and became field director for a Florida congressman's campaign for the U.S. Senate. Florida was a foreign area with two separate campaigns: one in the cosmopolitan Miami-Fort Lauderdale area and the other in the more rural, southern regions. He considered accepting a job in Washington because the congressman expected to win the race, but when he didn't, John returned to Berkeley. Upon his return, John received a call from Santa Cruz offering him a job. It was perfect for John because, although he had moved to Berkeley, he continued to spend his weekends in Santa Cruz.

In addition to working in the personnel office for Santa Cruz County, John maintained an active political life. Since his college days, he wrote on politics for newspapers and, for years, produced a regular column on the editorial page of the Sentinel. A prolific op-ed writer, he became a regular contributor to the Lavender Reader, a quarterly gay journal, and produced a prodigious amount for local political campaigns. A campaign would find him authoring fundraising letters for eight different candidates. He ghosted three ballot statements for the fall 2000 campaign and edited documents for SCAN and the Sierra Club.

In 1996, John hosted a weekly program, Talk of the Bay, on KUSP, where he invited public figures to discuss topics of political interest. Topics include water usage, transportation, and the effect of the Cisco development in San Jose on Santa Cruz County. Such public exposure invariably brought him in contact with others who thanked him for being brave enough to come out as openly gay and allow them to become more readily accepted. At the same time, John devoted his whole life to improving the community's quality of life, which may be his most enduring legacy.

In the course of all this, in 1995 John met John Flores, and they have been together twenty-eight years, fifteen of them married, which became legal in 2008. John Flores is an watercolor artist and recently retired from a forty year career in hair styling. "He is the best thing that happened to me – and as I have moved on to the state stage as a legislator and cabinet secretary, he's provided a good balance in life."

But John's heart is was always in Santa Cruz and it's future. "Santa Cruz is a unique mixture of beautiful environment, affordable surroundings, a university, proximity to San Francisco, and a small town feel that allows you to get to know people and appreciate their differences," he says. "We still rely upon many different people to make up the community. I worry about that being lost as the university grows, the Silicon Valley expands, and we provide new housing.

Author's note

All communities depend upon citizens to participate

in the many commissions, boards, and electoral offices to function. Santa Cruz has a disproportionate number of such concerned citizens. City Council meetings occasionally have large crowds and have moved from Chamber offices to the Civil Auditorium. John Laird not only participated in many local organizations and devoted innumerable hours to volunteering, he successfully ran for office. He was one of the first gay men to become the mayor of a city in the United States, served six years in the State Assembly, eight years as a Cabinet Secretary for Governor Jerry Brown, and is in his third year representing the Central Coast in the State Senate.

Coyote Thinking, metal sculpture by Daniel O. Stolpe

Mountain Girl's Acid Test Diploma

BENDING TIME, MAKING MAGIC, LONG STRANGE TRIP, THE BIG BLUR, FANTASY UNBOUND: ELECTRIC KOOL-AID ACID TEST REDUX; HISTORY AS ACID TRIP; ACID TRIP AS HISTORY

By Geoffrey Dunn

50 years ago Santa Cruz hosted a critical moment in counterculture history. Many of the participants are returning to celebrate the golden anniversary this week.

Who knew? I mean who could have known, really? Maybe some of them did, maybe Kesey, because he seemed to have the big vision, and perhaps even a sense of cosmic history—he was "Captain Flag" after all, the literary "Swashbuckler" and "Chief"—but it took far more than one heartbeat and one big persona for the moon and the planets and the stars to align so perfectly, so opportunistically, in such a crystalline fashion that cold Soquel night in November of 1965, precisely fifty years ago—my god, it's been a full half-century!—but align they did.

The Spread is gone, and the ranch house and the chicken coops and whatever else there was, and the condos and track homes have come to that sacred ground in the western watershed of Rodeo Gulch, which few Santa Cruzans realize—even those who have lived here forever—passes directly to the sea, into Corcoran Lagoon, a direct link to the grand Pacific, the great force that lured so much of that energy and consciousness and courage, yes courage, to the western shores, because the Pranksters who assembled that night at the Spread were courageous in ways that we today cannot fully fathom, bold if not always fearless, breaking through, going places, crashing beyond the various doors of perception, to borrow Aldous Huxley's phrase, trying to plow through the mind-numbing blue-window conformity of the postwar American night.

It's all connected—the holy sacred earth, the watersheds, our dreams, our souls, our pasts, our destinies. That was a part of their continued discovery, their psychic journey toward something further, their collective mission to save the soul and the minds of a generation…

But back to the Spread—located just above Soquel Drive near the junction of Mattison Lane, catty-corner from what is today the Silver Spur Restaurant—it was there on that fateful Saturday night in late 1965 that what has been identified as the "First Acid Test" ever was staged with some of the major cultural figures of the era: Kesey, as in the novelist Ken Kesey, celebrated author of One Flew Over Over the Cuckoo's Nest and Sometimes a Great Notion; the Beat poet Allen Ginsberg, author of Howl and Kaddish; Neal Cassady of On the Road fame who steered the Pranksters across America and into the naked cosmos; Kay Kesey, the Chief's wife and mother of three of his children (Larry McMurtry called her the glue that held it all together); and Ginsberg's lover and poet, Peter Orvlosky, along with his brother Julius.

Many of the Merry Pranksters, Keseys' wild inner-circle of psychic cosmonauts who had accompanied the author the year before on his bus called "Furthur" (or "Further," depending on the date), including Ken Babbs, Kesey's Prankster lieutenant, the "Intrepid Traveler," an ex-Marine and Vietnam War vet who actually first rented the Spread after relocating from San Juan Capistrano. Various members of that Palo Alto quasi-rock band the Warlocks, who in a matter of days would be known as the Grateful Dead—Jerry Garcia & Phil Lesh & Bob Weir & Pigpen & Bill Kreutzmann—attended with their friends "Foxy" Connie Bonner and "Faithful" Sue Swanson.

And perhaps the most endearing (and enduring) Prankster of them all—Carolyn Adams aka Mountain Girl (she "penetrated the Boys Club"!)—was rumored to have been there, Adams being described by Tom Wolfe in The Electric Kool-Aid Acid Test as "a tall girl, big and beautiful, with dark brown hair flowing down to her shoulders," mother of another of Kesey's kids ("Sunshine") and later Garcia's wife.

Or was she there? That's the rub. Maybe she was and maybe she wasn't. No one is quite sure. My buddy Lee Quarnstrom—former San Jose Mercury columnist, lifelong Prankster and author of a thoroughly enjoyable memoir entitled When I was a Dynamiter (see sidebar)—thinks she was there, he's pretty sure she was—so is Babbs—but who knows? Mountain Girl herself doesn't remember (she has said that she may have been back with her family for Thanksgiving that weekend, though I have definitively placed her in San Francisco, with Kesey,) and, other Pranksters, well, they aren't sure, either. If nothing else she was there in spirit, her energy a critical component of the Prankster tribe, its psychic gestalt.

At one point when I pressed Quarnstrom for details of the evening—the music, the guest list, to the point, I am sure of being a pest—he wrote me back that "frankly I cannot remember who all was at the Spread that evening, nor whether the whole band [the Warlocks] was there or just a few. Fifty years super-impose either a golden hue or a thick fog over many memories…I doubt whether this is all that helpful to you, but my mental exercises in 1965 were often too strenuous to help me remember that party clearly."

Babbs, for one, remembered it as a Halloween party. "It's all a myth now anyway," he said laughing that deep wild Intrepid Traveler laugh of his. "Tell it however you want."

So it goes. I have now assembled nearly two-dozen accounts of the evening and what led up to it—in writing, in conversation—and I suppose what emerges is more of an abstract painting than a precise photo-like rendition of history in the making. My sources were all high on LSD and weed and who knows what else.

Plus, like Lee said, it's been fifty fucking years. The hue is indeed golden, if not a little tarnished. Myths have been created and legends destroyed. The historical narrative of the last half-century has been warped, carpet bombed and digitized. Moreover, one of the mottos of Kesey & Co. was "never trust a Prankster," which adds yet another degree of difficulty to what is already a challenging task. So take this all with that proverbial grain of salt, or better yet, with that even more anti-proverbial tab of whatever it is that gets you there.

Let us start this tale with the Hip Pocket Bookstore, mid-1960s downtown Santa Cruz (located in the St. George Hotel complex, near where the Santa Cruz Coffee Roasting Company is today). It is tempting to say it all began there, but instead of envisioning it as a beginning, let us view it as an entrée into a cultural cataclysm, as a time & place where social magic and cultural alchemy took place.

And please allow me one small caveat: I get sick of people describing Santa Cruz as a "sleepy, conservative town" before the arrival of the university, mostly because I was a kid here then with roots stretching back to the 19th century, and Santa Cruz was far more complex and multi-faceted than such easy historical bromides suggest. There were other hip places in Santa Cruz before then, most notably the Sticky Wicket, a cool and very hip coffee shop first located downtown and that later moved out to Aptos (and which played a supporting role in this tale). And there were plenty of hip people. The war in Vietnam was raging and an entire generation of young American was rising up against it. Both Cabrillo College and UCSC had opened and the Free Speech Movement was going off in Berkley. The shifts of change were already in motion.

That said, there were strong forces of conservatism here at the time—members of the John Birch Society were on the Santa Cruz City School Board when I was a kid—and in the landmark presidential election of 1964, while this wasn't quite Goldwater Country, the Santa Cruz Sentinel actually endorsed him—whew!—calling him a "moderate." At precisely the same time that the Hip Pocket was opening, in September of 1964, Ronald Reagan—yes that Ronald Reagan!—came to Santa Cruz for a series of speaking engagements on behalf of Goldwater (who was well to the right of Attila the Hun) that included a mass rally for Goldwater at, dig this, the Santa Cruz High Auditorium.

So that's the firmament that Peter Demma and Ron Bevirt, the two principals of the Hip Pocket, were entering when they took out an ad in the very same Sentinel in September of that year with just blank space (I always wondered if the Sentinel censored the image) and a notice at the bottom of the ad announcing the unveiling of a legendary (and controversial) sculpture by Ron Boise and, dig this, a book signing by none other than Ken Kesey autographing his new novel Sometimes a Great Nation (sic—that must have been a Freudian slip by someone at the always literate Sentinel) and the "Intrepid Traveler's Merry Band." Which means that Kesey and the Pranksters had been here en masse more than a year before the First Acid Test.

Demma and Bevirt were clearly going against the tide. The Santa Cruz Polk's Directory for 1964-65 listed Demma as the bookstore's "Director," Bevirt as the "Hassler; " Patricia Ann Dutton as "Assistant Nexologist"; and Albert Smullin as being in charge of "Books for the Imagination." A paid advertisement in the same directory proclaims that the Hip Pocket sold "Books for Cowboys."

Demma, who passed away this past summer, was a key figure in the story as well. A native of Oakland, like many of the Beats and Pranksters, he had spent some time in the military and merchant marines, before lighting down on Perry Lane in Palo Alto, where his sister was living, and he came into contact with Kesey and iconic Beat legend Neal Cassady.

Demma once told me that he and Cassady, who loved Santa Cruz, would scoot over Highway 17 for quick visits to the beach and Boardwalk, and then return to Perry Lane. Demma also said that it was Cassady who first brought him to Santa Cruz and that he felt it was his "destiny" to own a bookshop, like a preternatural calling, and he had enlisted a close pal from the Kesey circle, Ron Bevirt—another ex-military guy in the Pranksters who had been stationed at Ford Ord—to join him in his bibliophile dreams. He hired Cassady to work there, too, and also Quarnstrom. It was a very cool place to hang.

While there was an article-with-picture earlier in the summer announcing the new downtown business, the Sentinel didn't exactly go out of its way to promote the Hip Pocket's grand opening in October of 1964. In fact, the lone mention of the store's unveiling came on the cops-and-robbers page the following day, where it was noted that someone from Big Sur attending the event was arrested on a "dope charge" for carrying a bottle of "shredded marijuana" and some pills that were "thought to be dangerous narcotics." It also noted that the unruly crowd assembled had the audacity to block Pacific Avenue and that the cops had been forced to break up the gathering and move the onlookers to the sidewalk.

Let me note with no small amount of pride—and dare

I say a certain amount of surprise—that the one welcoming mention in the Sentinel of that fateful event came in a notice written by my late (and highly eccentric) aunt, Estrella Stagnaro, who quoted E.P. Whipple with a nautical theme ("Books are lighthouses erected in the great sea of time") and which celebrated the "lovely" Hip Pocket's arrival in the community. She noted: "The Owners welcome you at all times!"

Perhaps so, but Santa Cruz did not really welcome the Hip Pocket. For its less than two-year run downtown, the place was embedded with controversy. From the very get-go, Ron Boise's statue, entitled "Runic"—a pair of nude figures, a man and a woman, pounded out of sheet metal and placed above the Hip Pocket sign (which Boise also crafted)—became an immediate cause célèbre downtown. (Quarnstrom remembers that a woman living in the St. George had a fit over the fact that a nekkid sheet-metal ass was blocking her view).

Boise was yet another critical figure in this drama, and, for an all-too-brief moment, a significant artistic force in the counterculture movement in California. Earlier that year, his sheet-metal nudes (part of a series he called Kama Sutra were featured in a show at the avant-garde North Beach Vorpal Art Gallery) had become a target for the gendarmes. San Francisco cops actually seized nearly a dozen of the sculptures, the show was shut down, and Muldoon Elder, the gallery's owner, was arrested for obscenity. The ensuing trial brought Boise lots of publicity (and Elder an acquittal by jury.)

Boise's next move was to come to Santa Cruz. The same summer that the Hip Pocket was opening for business, Boise had a show at the aforementioned Sticky Wicket featuring his Kama Sutra sculptures and also had works in a show sponsored by the Cabrillo Music Festival. He had moved with his girlfriend Space Daisy (a member of the Merry Pranksters and later Quarnstrom's wife) out to the Spread in Soquel. (Boise was a pal of my dad's because, among other things they had in common, they both had been sheet-metalsmiths in the Navy and my old man either loaned or gave him a bunch of tools that he had "appropriated" from the U.S. Government after World War II.)

Although the Boise statues were an affront to local conservatives tastes, an obscenity case had already failed against him, so the local powers-that-be waited until some nude images by celebrated New Mexico artist Walter Chappell graced the walls of the Bookshop. In the fall of 1965, Santa Cruz County District Attorney Richard Pease (pressured heavily by the brass in the Santa Cruz Police Department) slapped obscenity charges on Demma and Bevirt, which were followed by a string of wild-eyed headlines in the Sentinel. Pease proclaimed that "there will be a substantial number of people who will testify that they were outraged" by Chappell's images.

Apparently not that many. Only one local—Robert Husband, president of the then-ultra-conservative Santa Cruz Art League—testified against the photos. Several, however, took the stand in their favor. The local conservative power structure was shocked—and more than a little ticked—when Judge Harry Brauer dismissed the obscenity charges in a preliminary hearing based on First Amendment findings— much to the dismay of many, including the Sentinel's resident "liberal" columnist Wally Trabing, who acknowledged that he "was one who wanted to see a guilty verdict." Et tu, Wally?

That ruling came on Friday, November 26—the day before the celebrated "happening" at the Spread.

Some have speculated that the First Acid Test held the following night in Soquel was a celebration of the court's ruling in favor of the Hip Pocket. As Quarnstrom notes in When I Was a Dynamiter (and as he explained to me in even more detail in conversation and via email), it most certainly was not. But it undoubtedly added some additional joy to the festivities.

Quarnstrom had hooked up with Kesey and his band in La Honda after writing an article for the San Mateo Times about the author and his latest novel, Sometimes a Great Notion. Quarnstrom soon quit his gig, collected unemployment checks, moved into a cabin in La Honda near Kesey & Co., and was later arrested with Kesey, Cassady and a host of other Pranksters for marijuana possession in April of 1965.

Kesey and the Pranksters, who had returned to La Honda after their cross-country journey on "Furthur," where they had hosted several acid-fueled "happenings," were wanting to bring their show—and their experiences with mind-expanding drugs—to the masses. In the words of Wolfe, Kesey had intended to develop "a ritus, often involving music, dance, liturgy, sacrifice, to achieve an objectified and stereotyped expression of the original spontaneous religious experience." Kesey wanted to bend time. Kool-Aid spiked with LSD became sacramental wine of the ritus.

The Pranksters were ready to hit the road once more. The scene in La Honda was beginning to feel cooped up— both literally and figuratively (Quarnstrom says that the septic tank there had filled and sewage was backed up into the kitchen sink)—and there were too many Hell's Angels hanging around, so that "one by one, the Pranksters living in La Honda began a Diaspora that brought me and a few others down the coast to Santa Cruz."

By November of 1965, Quarnstrom, along with other Pranksters and associates (including the entire Kesey family, Babbs, Demma, Mountain Girl, Bevirt and his girlfriend Space

Daisy had moved into the run-down ranch house in Soquel that Babbs says he had first rented when he was relocating from San Juan Capistrano.

According to T. Wolfe, the Pranksters had been looking for a larger, public venue in Santa Cruz to hold their embryonic Acid Test, but the "Pranksters were not the best mechanics at things like hiring a hall." So the Spread was a last-minute fallback location.

Word of the party was passed through the likes of Hassler and Bevirt and Demma and Quarnstrom at the Hip Pocket. Wolfe asserts that writer and artist Norman Hartweg used some cue cards to make up signs (a fact disputed by others) to put up in the bookshop asking "Can You Pass the Acid Test?" A handbill advertising the event—replete with a single eye and a reference to the Warlocks and Babbs showed up on eBay several years ago (some dispute its authenticity as well), but since it's the only surviving artifact of the event—no photos, no film, no audio tapes—I am holding on to its verity even if it was conjured after-the-fact. It's all we have.

Roughly fifty people showed up during the evening. One of them, Carole Kettmann, a 16-year-old junior at Santa Cruz High School, had befriended Quarnstrom and others at the Hip Pocket and was one of those outside the Prankster inner-circle who attended the event. "I loved hanging out at the Hip Pocket," she recalls. "People were always fun and interesting. They all had this great vibe. I felt the excitement."

The Pranksters had set up a film projector and were showing sequences from the footage accumulated on their cross-country bus trip. Music was blasting, there was a light show—and there was LSD (which, it should be duly noted, was legal at the time). In Dennis McNally's landmark history of the Dead, What a Long Strange Trip, he notes that Phil Lesh "would always recall the capsules they took that night, completely transparent except for the tiniest of scratches on the inner surface that marked the LSD that was their transport to another world. He spent much of the evening staring at the stars." Kettmann remembers that "the acid was really good. It was pure." Any other details from the night elude her—but she apparently passed the test.

Some people remember the Warlocks setting up in the living room. Others are not so sure. Lesh recalled trying to wrangle an electric guitar from Kesey. After staring at him long enough, Kesey eventually, albeit reluctantly, gave up the guitar. Bob Weir remembered staying close to Ginsberg and tripping out on whatever he had to say. In The Grateful Dead: Vanguard of a New Generation, Hank Harrison says that the music played that night wasn't "rock and roll, just prankster music." Garcia (soon to be dubbed "Captain Trips") would tell Blair Jackson that he and the other Warlocks "plugged all our stuff in [at the Spread] and played for about a minute. Then we all freaked out. But we made a good impression on everybody in that minute, so we were invited to the next one."

Boise, who was staying in his truck at the Spread, had made a large contraption called a Thunder Machine out of a 1958 Chevy that Quarnstrom had crashed. Boise apparently made several of these devices, which had been painted in psychedelic Day-Glo designs by acclaimed Santa Cruz artist Joe Lysowski (whose father worked as a cook at the wharf). The machines were of nondescript shape—a large glob of sheet metal—with wires strung tightly like a guitar, so that the machine itself, according to Quarnstrom, "could be pounded on, plucked, shouted into and climbed."

Cassady rapped into a microphone; Ginsberg chanted. Of the party, Weir would later say, "It was actually better than realizing my dreams."

At the end of the evening, according to Wolfe's account,

which is as reliable as any, at about 3 a.m., a "thing happened." Those people who had come strictly for the party, the "beano" as Wolfe dubbed it, had split, leaving just the core group connected one way or other to the inner-circle.

The two power forces among them, Kesey and Ginsberg, yin and yang, found themselves, figuratively and literally, on different sides of the rooms, with everyone who remained circled around "these two poles like on a magnet," and the Kesey people pulled closer to the young, muscular novelist him, and the Ginsberg people toward the older, long-haired poet—"the super-West and the super-East"—and suddenly the subject turned to the war raging in Vietnam. Wolfe goes on:

Kesey gives his theory of whole multitudes of people joining hands in a clump and walking away from the war. Ginsberg said all these things, these wars, were the result of misunderstandings. Nobody who was doing the fighting ever wanted to be doing it, and if only everybody could sit around in a friendly way and talk it out, they could get to the root of their misunderstanding and settle it—and then from the rear of the Kesey contingent came the voice of the only man in the room who had been within a thousand miles of the war, Babbs, saying, "Yes. it's all so very obvious."

It's all so very obvious...How magical that comment seemed at that moment! The magical eighth hour of acid—how clear it all now was—Ginsberg had said it, Babbs, the warrior, had certified it, and it had all built to this, and suddenly everything was so...very clear.

And that is how the very First Acid Test, held at the Spread in Soquel—in the heart of Santa Cruz County—ended, not with a roar, but on a quiet magical moment. Something heavy had happened—you had to be there to experience it, to feel it, to grasp it—but like a pebble tossed into a quiet mountain lake, its ripples would be felt on distant shores for years and decades to come.

It hadn't really been a fully public event—far from it, as Wolfe noted, "it didn't really...reach out into the world" —it had been contained and not all that different from similar parties thrown by the Pranksters and Warlocks in La Honda, but the happening in Soquel would serve as a test run, a prototype, for many more to come.

The Pranksters and the newly named Grateful Dead took their Acid Tests on the road immediately thereafter. The next one was a week later in San Jose—following a concert by the Rolling Stones at the San Jose Civic Auditorium—ensued in quick succession by similar events at Muir Beach, Palo Alto, Portland, and then, in mid-January, a three-day "Trips Festival" at the Longshoreman's Hall in San Francisco that had been organized and promoted by Stewart Brand, later of Whole Earth Catalog fame.

At the door was Bill Graham, who, according to Mountain Girl, made sure that everyone who came in had paid for a ticket. When Garcia wanted to let friends in for free, Graham became unhinged. Garcia recalled that the only person who wasn't high that day was Graham. As Graham liked to say, it wasn't about the money—it was about the money. The commodification of the counterculture and getting high had begun.

There was one hitch to the Trips Festival. On the "Acid Test" day of the event, Kesey had to come incognito—he wore a space suit and helmet, while his voice blasted over the sound system—because he and Mountain Girl had been busted a few days earlier on a rooftop in San Francisco a second time for pot (he had just been sentenced to six months in county jail for his first offense, promising the judge that he was moving permanently to Santa Cruz). Now, he was being threatened with up to five years in prison. The Feds were out to get him. By January of 1966, Ken Kesey was viewed by the United States government to be a very dangerous man.

Shortly thereafter, Kesey faked his suicide and headed for Mexico (driven there by Boise). The FBI came to the Hip Pocket and the Spread looking for the outlaw author, but everyone played dumb. Many of the Pranksters followed Kesey down to Mazatlan later that year after Kesey had called Demma from Puerto Vallarta to tell him of his whereabouts. Not long after, Mountain Girl was placed on two-years probation, the Hip Pocket went bankrupt, Boise died at the age of 34 from congenital heart failure, the scene at the Spread broke up, and Kesey—having served out a plea-bargained jail sentence on lesser charges in San Mateo County—moved back to his home base in Oregon. And on October 24, 1968—a week before the election of Richard Nixon as President of the United Stares—LSD was made illegal.

The party was over. Sort of. Rumor has it that the Grateful Dead played a few more gigs.

There's a poem I love by Jack Spicer called "Imaginary Elegies: IV" that I thought a lot about while researching and conducting interviews for this story. It concludes:

> *Upon the old amusement pier I watch*
> *The creeping darkness gather in the west.*
> *Above the giant funhouse and the ghosts*
> *I hear the seagulls call. They're going west*
> *Toward some great Catalina of a dream*
> *Out where the poem ends.*
> *But does it end?*
> *The birds are still in flight. Believe the birds.*

I do believe the birds. Stories do not end. Narratives do.

Endings are the conceit of storytellers and morticians.

Earlier this week, as I was rereading The Electric Kool-Aid Acid Test, not far from the where the Hip Pocket Bookstore opened its doors below Ron Boise's two naked sculptures in the mid-1960s, I watched a group of young kids, the same age as many of those who staged and attended the First Acid Test fifty years ago, their necks bent downward and their eyes glued to electronic devices made at sweatshops in China, all utterly oblivious to the glories and the other human beings around them.

The scene at once disturbed and frightened me. I felt a little unnerved.

I thought of Kesey and Cassady and Garcia and Mountain Girl and all the Pranksters who struggled to break free from their era's imposing conformities that shackled their lives. What I hoped for at that moment was that all of us—not only those kids I had just encountered downtown, but indeed all of us—could somehow find our way through those dangerous doors of perception and discover the inner Prankster that still lurks inside us all.

I decided to go to the beach at 4th Avenue where I encountered a glorious autumn sunset, neon hues of orange and indigo shooting into the heavens. And there on the horizon, yes!, the birds were still in flight.

Geoffrey Dunn's most recent book is Santa Cruz Is in the Heart: Volume II. He is the 2015 Santa Cruz County Artist of the Year.

Party Pranksters:
Top Left: Mountain Girl or Carmen Garcia, Lee Quarnstrom, ?, ?, Babbs'
wife, Ken Babbs
Lower Left. Jami Cassady, Ron Polte, "Ace of Cups" Denise Kaufman

HIDDEN DELL
By Elizabeth Hansen (nee Hutchinson)

Hidden Dell is a few acres hugging Soquel Creek as it tumbles down the west facing slope of the Santa Cruz Mountains, winding its way towards Soquel Cove on Monterey Bay. It is an old homestead nestled into a Douglas Fir and Coast Redwood Forest where the meadows are dotted with huge apple and persimmon trees celebrating the flow of seasons with their flowers, buds and fruits reveling through foggy mornings and blue-sky days.

An aged barn anchors the property on a circular driveway connecting the other tiny wooden, dilapidated buildings housing the Skolnick clan and a few others who find the low rents and country lifestyle desirable.

These coastal hill environs were heavily populated in previous generations by those of a leftist political persuasion; labor organizers, old communists, people who worked for the societal "common good". The owners in 1966 were just that. Emily, a Des Moines heiress and political activist, and Alec Skolnick, a San Mateo psychiatrist, and Stanford University adjunct professor, had been long time proprietors of the land. They had recently completed building their own new home on the property, set off across the meadow from the old barn and attendant housing where their children Marcia, Mark and Ellen all had dwellings at their disposal.

The Skolnicks had lived two doors down the street from my family in San Mateo, but we were not acquainted. Mark had graduated from my high school, Aragon, two years before me and at a ceremony for the graduates that year his name rang out through the gymnasium where it was held, sending an incredible wave of energy through me, portending a connection I could not imagine.

The summer of 1965 some friends and I dropped by Mark's Berkeley apartment where he was ensconced on his summer break from Princeton University. By the time of my graduation from high school in 1966 I was "seeing" Mark and eventually he convinced my parents that I would be "safe" if allowed to spend the night at Hidden Dell—and so began our summer of Love.

Soquel Creek carved through the property leaving stony, sandy beaches alongside its banks and the summer was initiated by damming up a swimming hole. It was the favorite place to hang out for residents and visitors alike, offering sufficient privacy to lay out naked soaking up the sun until a swim in the cooling creek pool beckoned. It was a languid, sensual interlude in an otherwise revolutionary social time.

Trying to find something affordable to eat in the Santa Cruz – Soquel area in 1966 was a real trial. Hamburgers of questionable quality were widely available and the only vegetarian options were the ubiquitous "grilled cheese sandwich" composed of squishy white bread and Velveeta, or "American" cheese. It was bleak. Salad, if available, consisted of iceberg lettuce and blue cheese or thousand island dressing. As I had been an activist for the Ceasar Chavez farm workers in high school, handing out leaflets at school encouraging folks to boycott iceberg lettuce... I did not eat iceberg lettuce.

Political awareness and activism had been a big part of my life throughout high school where I participated regularly in student government. Outside of school activities I participated in electoral politics, fair housing and farmworker issues, civil rights advocacy, and anti-Vietnam War activities.

I was headed to UC Berkeley where only two years before the Free Speech Movement erupted, its remnants smoldered and reignited into a conflagration against the war in Vietnam. All of this was very compelling for me, and I did not stand on the sidelines, instead attended meetings, conferences, protest marches against the War and draft and for People's Park. I was thoroughly convinced that by raising awareness and educating people with the "facts" that everyone would come to agree on the need to improve the society in which we all participated. Ah youth!

Fueled by hormones no doubt, the summer of 1966 offered me a new type of raised awareness initiated by falling in love. Hidden Dell was the incubator and took on an ideal glow through my rose-colored glasses. I was still living at home and only visited on occasion during the summer of 1966. Mark struggled to finish his thesis that summer to graduate the following year from Princeton. It turned out to be a moot point, since he never graduated from Princeton. By fall I had moved into my UC Berkeley dorm.

In 1967-8 we were weekenders and summer residents; visiting the Catalyst for a coffee or soft drink surrounded by plants beneath the glass ceiling, looking for books and records, going to the Renaissance Faire, shopping for fruits and vegetables at the local farm stands, sleeping under the starry night sky, making music, and welcoming visitors who happened by.

One day Lauren Hutton, the "IT" model then, came riding into the property astride a big motorcycle driven by a capable young man. They "had heard" about this place and wanted to see what was "happening" …all the way from New York! Phil Bliss, a scion of a prominent Santa Cruz family, and his girlfriend Joyce Cole, an acquaintance of mine from high school, made an appearance, as well as my high school best friend, Karen Kromhout, a student at U. C. Santa Cruz at the time. Several Princeton men were visitors, including Harold

Arnold and his girlfriend Tara. Ralph Abraham's name came up frequently but the opportunity to hook up never presented itself. I remember meeting another Princeton fellow, Doug Wolfe, in the woods hanging out with a group. He seemed a bit unhinged, and he did go crazy the following year. People would drop by to visit Marcia, or Ellen, or other tenants. Sam Buchanan, Marsha's friend, lived in the barn for a time, helping make it habitable.

Music played incessantly on our guitars, turn tables and the air waves as radio played all the new rock and roll. The Byrds, Eight Miles High, Turn, Turn, Turn, Otis Redding, Dock of the Bay. Life at Hidden Dell was a revelation for me, a suburban girl all of 18 who had a precocious political awareness and love of rock and roll, but was not versed in milking goats, keeping chickens, organic gardening, stocking the "icebox" with blocks of ice, etc., let alone the constant exposure to such a wide variety of people!

A resident married couple who had a very settled domestic life in the biggest rental house fascinated me. They were serious students of Rosicrucianism. He was finishing his thesis for his PhD in Classics, and we spent time talking about metaphysics and mysticism, among other things. While marijuana was widely in use on the property it was not part of these people's regime, although one could never have accused them of being 'straight', a term that was generally used to describe people who lived outside the burgeoning alternative, stoned, rock and roll, political zeitgeist. Late one afternoon as the light slanted through the windows, he drew my attention to his magic cat 5 feet in front of me. It jumped, twisting straight into the air, and disappeared. I was dumbstruck and still cannot believe this happened...but I know it did. He vanished in front of my eyes.

One day a very small man in monk's robes arrived on

the property. He had a terrible case of hiccups. I felt sorry for him. He did not speak English well but eventually, as the days wore on, it became evident that he had had these hiccups for several months. He seemed to be expending a lot of energy on NOT freaking out about the hiccups (or something else), but clearly, he was suffering from some kind of repressed hysteria or anxiety (IMHO).

I tried all sorts of things to help him overcome the hiccups. The tricks we all learned as kids; frightening someone, startling them, jumping up and down pounding the opposite ear, etc. did not work. Some hilarity ensued with each of these failed attempts. Finally, through demonstration, I got him to try the drinking sips out of the opposite lip of a glass of water trick. Miraculously it worked. His hiccups subsided. His relief was profound.

Later Emily explained that she worked with a peace group that was sponsoring this Vietnamese monk's American speaking tour and he was sheltering at Hidden Dell. In Vietnam, among other activities, he had led a huge group of children in a long peace march across Vietnam as a protest against the war that was ravaging their country at the time and did until 1975. It had been a very dangerous endeavor and did not put him in good graces with the Vietnamese government or American Military. The hiccups had come on as the stress of his dangerous position increased. We were finally able, after days of trying, to relieve the hiccups with a little water, laughter, compassion, and a safe place. He was among helpful people; he was going to be alright. He stayed on at Hidden Dell for a while before heading out on his speaking tour. Thich Nhat Hanh was his name, he went on to becomes a major and much beloved Buddhist teacher in America and around the world.

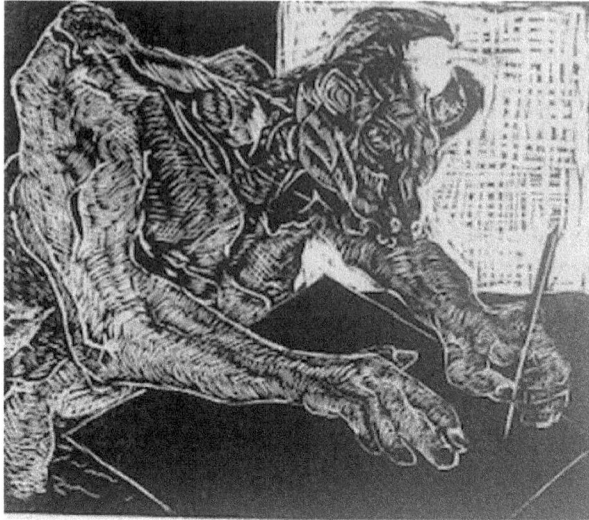

Coyote Creating by Daniel O. Stolpe

POEM FOR DAN STOLPE
By Yaryan

*At the beginning
and end of the world
Coyote the Trickster can be found.*

*From Native American legend and myth,
the archetypal Coyote figure was responsible
for creating the earth
and considered fully capable of destroying it
at any given moment
in means of setting things right.*

*As the legendary Coyote does things his own way
and shakes up convention
so did the late Daniel O. Stolpe.
The artist*

who produced
on his own terms.
Creations
with exciting visual narratives
expressed mythical themes

.

In his painting and print studio,
Stolpe devoted himself completely to his vocation
as a painter and master printmaker for many moons

The Four Horsemen of the Apocalypse
an encounter with fear and chaos
Apocalypse and Cabalgaran
driving force of conflict and sensuality.
All of Stolpe's images prompt contemplation
of survival
In the physical world.

Through compelling use of color and design
the powerful myths of Coyote
the trickster
leap to life
because, while with us here
Stolpe set sights into the spirit world…and prompted us
to do the same
through magnificent visualizations

Stolpe learned valuable lessons from Coyote
who demonstrated, through humorous folly
and cleverness
how to survive

The artist attempted to bring unity

within the parameters of his own life
keep the lessons of Native American beliefs alive
inside of himself
in his work

the foundation of these beliefs grew
from the darkness and lightness
from early age to seasoned sage
he gained understanding and respect
for the sacredness of life

"Coyote's mission is to bring balance to the world," Stolpe
once said
Survival depends upon recognition of this balancing act
on both a personal and a societal level

Coyote
made
an indelible impression
on Stolpe's vocation.
Coyote's ability to adapt
to the changing forces of his environment
represented the will
and strength
always present
in Daniel O. Stolpe's visual storytelling
with a prolific body of brilliant art
destined to endure the ages

Note

Daniel O. Stolpe was a master printer and artist who founded Native Images Studio from 1979-2018 in Santa Cruz,

CA. His Art is exhibited nationally and also collected by numerous institutions, including UCSC. Much of his artwork is relative to Shamanism, being one of the intermediaries between ordinary and non-ordinary states of reality, a seer and a healer. Through Art,

T. Mike Walker, Daniel O. Stolpe, and Dan Yaryan

Stolpe opened the Shadow, the dark side of his persona, to find universal truths. Like Stolpe, Ralph was a member of the Coyote Tribe—like us, Daniel and Ralph howled at the Moon! For more information visit ordinary and non-ordinary states of reality, a seer and a healer. Through Art, Stolpe opened the Shadow, the dark side of his persona, to find universal truths. Like Stolpe, Ralph was a member of the Coyote Tribe—like us, Daniel and Ralph howled at the Moon!

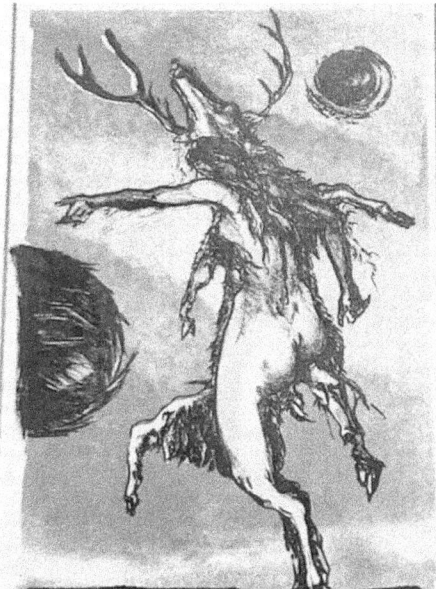

Spirit Dancer by Daniel O. Stolpe

SHEET METAL DREAMS: RUNIC FOR MANKIND KAMA SUTRA BLUES
The Transformative Art and All-Too Short Beatific Life of Sculptor Ron Boise

by Geoffrey Dunn

The arrival of a large, sheet-metal sculpture in downtown Santa Cruz during September of 1964 generated an appreciable buzz along Pacific Avenue, one that reverberated throughout the entire community and along the Central Coast.

Ron Boise—a young, iconoclastic and extremely talented sculptor quickly gaining national and, even, international renown—was set to unveil his latest work, "Runic for Mankind," above the newly opened Hip Pocket Bookstore on Pacific Avenue, in the St. George Hotel near where Bookshop Santa Cruz stands today.

Approaching 12-feet tall and constructed out of copper sheeting, the sculpture depicted a man and a woman, both nude, casually covering their genitalia with clasped hands. "His sculpture was extremely sensual," the San Francisco Examiner art critic Richard Groom. "The rendering of flesh and texture of the sheet metal made you forget they were scraps of metal at all. He had a sensitive line in his work that made all the metal personages seem to have a personality all their own."

My late friend Lee Quarnstrom—the former San Jose Mercury columnist who cut his teeth with novelist Ken Kesey's Merry Pranksters—was then living with Boise at a rural compound called "The Spread" out in Soquel, which also included other Prankster stalwarts, including Kesey. Quarnstrom recalled that soon after the sculpture's installation a woman living in the hotel "had a fit that a sheet-metal ass was blocking her view."

It is almost impossible for recent arrivals in Santa Cruz to grasp how conservative the local community was at that time. In the landmark presidential election of 1964, while this wasn't quite Goldwater Country, the Santa Cruz Sentinel actually endorsed him, calling him a "moderate." At precisely the same time of the Boise unveiling, Ronald Reagan—later to be governor and, eventually, president—came to Santa Cruz for a series of speaking engagements on behalf of Goldwater that included a mass rally at the Santa Cruz High Auditorium.

This was the milieu in which Boise, his sculpture, and his colorful Prankster friends arrived in Santa Cruz. In a very real sense, he had taken "Runic for Mankind" into the belly of the beast.

The imposing structure, gazing down upon those doing their day-to-day business on Pacific Avenue, became an immediate cause célèbre in the local community. It was possessed of a serene, beatific humanity at a time when the United States was attempting to bomb Vietnam "back into the Stone Age."

Boise had created a talisman for the bourgeoning counterculture on the West Coast and tapped into its zeitgeist. His statue forced us all to strip bare our souls, to render ourselves naked before the elemental truths and beauties of the universe.

The artist Ronald Lee Boise was born on December 22, 1931, in the high prairielands of Brush, Colorado, just west of the Nebraska border. His father ran a service station, while his mother was an art teacher. (For reasons unknown, his family changed its surname from "Bosse" to "Boise" at some point in the aftermath of World War II.)

Following high school, Boise briefly attended Colorado

State Teachers College, before entering the U.S. Navy in 1949. He was stationed on the isle of Guam, during which time he served as a welder, mechanic and sheet metalsmith at the Naval Special Warfare Unit One. Much to his lifelong chagrin, he was forced to stay two years longer than expected because of the Korean War.

With educational funds in his pocket from the GI Bill, he studied at El Camino College in Torrance, continued his studies for two more years in Mexico City, then returned to the South Bay in booming post-war Los Angeles, to which various members of his family had also relocated.

In 1957, the 25-year-old Boise landed a job as director of the Exodus Galleries Coffeehouse in San Pedro, where he first began showing his work. At the same time, he staged several experimental film and poetry readings; avant-garde jazz and theatre. He made rough-hewn furniture and brought in "exotic coffees" as part of the daily fare.

The Exodus began generating local and regional press. In one early profile of Boise appearing in the San Pedro News Pilot, the artist was described as a "red-bearded, sandal-shod coffee-house proprietor." He was already identifying himself as a maverick and member of the Beat Generation. When asked what that meant to him, he opined, "It's somebody who throws up his hands at [current] affairs, who sits around philosophizing about things like Buddhism."

More significantly, in respect to his personal artistic journey, he declared, "I am trying to develop myself as a sculptor, but I know I'm not good enough to make a living at it, so I started this coffee house nine months ago with $35 in my pocket....If you really want to know how this place is different from other places where people spend their leisure time, you might say that, here, you will find people who still have faith in the intelligence of the common man."

Boise eventually became a popular and protean figure in the L.A art scene—a cultural moment that is wonderfully recounted by Hunter Drohojowska-Philp's Rebels in Paradise: The Los Angeles Art Scene and the 1960s.

Boise's work quickly switched from an amalgamation of source materials (bumpers, engine parts, frames, household appliances, and other hardware) to primarily sheet metal from automobiles. He preferred using the metal from 1950 and 1951 Fords. "I don't know what it is," he declared, "but the alloy they put into it during those years made the metal a lot stronger."

As for his seminal artistic influences, he claimed that his inspiration came in the early 1950s, while he was "doing some welding on a kid's hotrod and an architect dropped by and suggested that I try doing some abstract metal work. I tried and became hooked, and here I am." His creative energy, he said, "was part of my nature. I don't ask myself whether society will accept my work. I only ask myself whether I will accept it. Naturally, I do and wouldn't attempt anything else."

Boise briefly became a darling of the L.A. media, including long-time film producer, and photographer Leland Auslender. A few years older than Boise, he worked in mainstream film production, but also made art house films. Auslender shot 16mm footage and large slides of Boise and his sculptures. He once told me that Boise was "the ultimate artist—he was able to pour his passion into his work. I was very much taken by him and liked him very much." (A portion of his early art documentary, "The Sculpture of Ron Boise" can still be found on YouTube.)

Boise was always refining (and redefining) his artistic medium. During his decade of artistic output (roughly 1957 to 1966), Boise's genre shifted from abstract geometric works to figurative sculptures (mostly of women, then to women and men in relation to each other—spiritually, emotionally, sexually.

By 1963, the peripatetic Boise was on the move again, headed north; by now, he had connected with a new lover, Emilia Espinosa Hazelip: a dark-eyed, free-spirited Catalan. A half-decade younger than Boise, she would serve as his muse during the most creative, if controversial, period of his life. In one account of the pair in the Palo Alto Times, Hazelip's presence was described thusly: "At [Boise's] side, alternately executing happy pirouettes or wild flamenco dance steps stood an exquisite fine-featured Spanish girl clad heavy-wooled [sic] serape and knee-high rawhide boots." She and Boise made a colorful—and culturally attractive—pair.

Boise purchased a converted, 1945 bread truck and moved through the emerging counter-cultural scenes in the greater San Francisco and Monterey Bay areas (from Tiburon south to the Peninsula, then Big Sur, and finally Santa Cruz.)

In late 1963, Boise began working on what would be called his Kama Sutra series: eleven small statues (roughly 20 inches in height) depicting various positions of sexual union as described in the ancient Hindu text of the same name. His muse had struck. "I fell in love," Boise acknowledged. "So I sculpted people in love. It felt right. It was a gift to my beloved."

By spring of the following year, Boise staged a Kama Sutra exhibit at the avant-garde Vorpal Art Gallery, in San Francisco's North Beach, which had been founded by the debonair artist and dealer Muldoon Elder earlier in the decade. Boise's show included eleven Kama Sutra works and fifteen other pieces, including life-size female nudes and a couple of off-beat musical instruments. The exhibit soon became a target for the San Francisco Police. The cops actually seized the Kama Sutra sculptures (they were forced to return them until a trial was held) and the 28-year-old Elder was arrested on obscenity charges.

The ensuing trial brought Boise and the Vorpal national publicity. After deliberating for merely six hours, the jury of 7 men and 5 women found that the sculptures were not obscene. Elder was acquitted—and triumphant.

Shortly thereafter, Boise returned to Santa Cruz. The same summer that the Hip Pocket was opening for business, Boise had a show at an early Santa Cruz coffee house called the Sticky Wicket and also had works in a show sponsored by the Cabrillo Music Festival. He had moved in with his Prankster friends to the Spread in Soquel, where he began making so-called Thunder Machines, painted by Santa Cruz artist Joe Lysowski, for the Pranksters' "Acid Test" events, featuring the Grateful Dead.

Boise's fame and notoriety, however, were relatively short-lived. While he held individual shows throughout the United States and Europe in the aftermath of the Kama Sutra controversy, his health deteriorated quickly. There were rumors of drug and alcohol abuse, and he and Hazelip parted ways. During the installation of a show of his in Dallas, he took ill and returned to Santa Cruz, where he died in May of 1966 at the age of 34, apparently of heart disease.

He had suffered from rheumatic fever as a child, and it may well have been that he died from rheumatic fever exacerbated by an infection. Posts on the internet claiming that he died of a drug overdose in Texas simply aren't true. That said, many in the community felt that he had not been properly diagnosed and given proper medical care.

He was buried by his parents at the Pacific Crest Cemetery in Redondo Beach, where he first made a name for himself as an artist in the L.A. art scene of the early 1960s.

A handful of posthumous shows were held in his honor in the years after, including one in Santa Cruz, but for a variety of reasons, his artistic impact on Western art and the counterculture was quickly swept away. He had no one to carry on his torch, and many works went underground or were lost or stolen.

His friend and attorney James Wolpman has loyally kept a web site in his honor (http://www.boiselifeworks.info), on which photographs of iconic sculptures (taken by another dear and loyal friend, the late Lars Speyer) can be viewed. Aside from that, I was not able to find a single piece of his work in any public museum or art gallery.

More than a half-century after his death, Boise's once national, even international, reputation has all but vanished. The famed iconic image, "Runic for Mankind," which graced Pacific Avenue in the mid-1960s, had first been moved, in 1966, to the roof of the Anchor Steam Beer brewery in San Francisco (where it was referred to as "theCouple,"), and then was gifted by brewery owner Fritz Maytag to an art collector in Arizona, where it resides quietly today.

"Rubric for Mankind" sculpture by Ron Boise

Ron Boise and Model

Ralph Abraham and his wife, Ray Gwyn Smith

CROISSANTS FORM THE BASIS FOR A COMMUNITY: GAYLE'S BAKERY
by Don Monkerud

Gayle's Bakery and its delicious baked goods reflect Gayle Ortiz's independence, creativity, and determination, rooted in her early family life. Gayle was born and raised in San Jose and grew up in a typical middle-class home; her father was the general manager of Carnation Milk, and her mother stayed at home. Her creativity came from her mother, who imparted a love of crafts to her. Her mother was always working on a creative project of some sort and couldn't sit still without knitting, sewing, or making things from paper. During the last part of her life, she made miniature dollhouses, a turn-of-the-century schoolhouse, and a millinery shop complete with tiny hats. Gayle inherited her mother's love of crafts and, for twenty years, made mosaic tables and other items from broken plates.

During Gayle's early years, her sister, four years older, was the good daughter, while Gayle was considered independent and wild. She ran away from home when she was four but called her mother and asked to be picked up after riding her bicycle as far as Los Gatos. She insisted on determining her own life and making her own decisions in high school and attributes this independent streak to her overprotective parents. Her father came from an Irish Catholic family of six who were always drinking and getting into some sort of trouble. Seeking to protect his daughters from the bad experiences of his own siblings, he kept a tight rein on his daughters. Although she was the vice president of her class and a cheerleader with good grades, Gayle felt stifled, chafing under the strict rules and yearning for independence.

"My dad kept a tight rein, and the tighter he got, the wilder I got," Gayle recounted. "The last half of my senior year, I met a biker in my class who was truly wild. My parents put their foot down and said I couldn't see him, which only made me want to see him more."

Her biker boyfriend joined the army after high school and called Gayle from Kentucky just before the finals of her freshman year in college. He was shipping out to Vietnam in three months and asked her to marry him. Although she was only 17 and needed her parents' approval, Gayle dropped out of school and went to Kentucky to marry. There, in a state where cousins marry cousins, her age was no problem, although she still recalls her discomfort at having to kiss the huge judge who was smoking a foul cigar when he read them their vows.

She spent four very exciting married years to become the normal one in her family. Her husband returned from Vietnam with malaria and "even more emotionally damaged than he was when he left." They lived in San Jose, where her husband bought a new motorcycle and began to take long motorcycle trips. Unannounced absences of a day or two grew into weeks. Gayle couldn't stand it. She moved in with a roommate when he was gone, and he reacted violently upon his return. She had him arrested.

Gayle had already met Joe Ortiz, who was dating her roommate, and he came back into her life after she split up with her husband. Joe had dropped out of law school and was painting houses when he accepted Gayle's invitation to dinner. He came to dinner and didn't leave. They moved to San Francisco where Joe returned to law school, only to find out why he had left in the first place. Restless, Joe moved to Colorado for two months with a friend to paint houses. When he returned, the landlord raised the rent on their Castrodistrict house from $300 to $900 a month, and they decided to move to Capitola, where Gayle vacationed as a child. Both of them commuted to San Francisco—Joe painting houses and Gayle waitressing—until she got a job in 1974 as a waitress at the Edgewater Restaurant in Santa Cruz. At that point, she had no idea that her life was about to change drastically as she soon forged a new life running a bakery.

Smoke billowed from the oven. The air grew thick with the smell of burning butter. If there had been a fire alarm, it would have awakened the whole neighborhood, jarred the windows, and screeched across the early dawn like a fire truck. Luckily, there was no fire, only the haunting failure of a batch of croissants.

Opening the door to the oven, Gayle discovered that her carefully placed layers of butter, interspersed coil by coil with rolled dough, had simply melted and run out onto the pan. The puny lumps of scorched dough didn't look anything like the picture in the cookbook. And she had followed the cookbook directions to the letter.

Why such a failure? She liked to bake too—cakes and cookies in high school, albeit with similar results—until she discovered boys. Now an adult, she knew how to follow a recipe and desperately wanted success.

She realized baking the perfect croissant would be difficult because she had never tasted a croissant. But she was determined to be successful, even though her baking career was somewhat of a fluke. When commuting to San Francisco to paint houses, Joe, now her husband, came home one day with a proposition from a chef who wanted to trade baking classes in exchange for Joe painting the cooking school. What would he do with cooking classes? Although the painting job didn't come through, Gayle jumped at the opportunity to take classes with Flo Baker, a well-known bakery chef at the time who later achieved national renown. For eight weeks, Gayle drove to the city every Thursday and made three or four pastries in the morning before driving home to her job as a cocktail waitress in the Crow's Nest at the Yacht Harbor.

Fortuitously, Gayle met the owner of Chez Panisse in Berkeley and discovered that Linda Sheer, the pastry chef, was going to Europe in the summer of 1976 and needed someone to take her place for several months. The task was daunting; she would be cooking for a well-known restaurant, rapidly gaining a reputation for California cuisine, but Gayle would be working with another woman, so the burden wouldn't fall entirely on her. Taking a leave of absence from the Crow's Nest, Gayle decided to try it. Two days into the job, the other woman had a nervous breakdown and left Gayle on her own. Despite long hours and hot ovens, Gayle discovered that she loved baking. She even mastered baking delicate croissants and decided to see where baking might lead. She returned home to Capitola and began baking to earn extra money, meeting some success baking cakes for local restaurants and stores.

"I got up every morning at 6 a.m., made croissants from the dough I'd made the day before, let them rest under tea towels, ate breakfast, put the croissants in the oven, and took a shower," Gayle said. "Then I'd go out and sell the croissants, getting back in time for my job at the Crow's Nest. I'd come home at 2 p.m. and start over, again making dough for the next day."

She began to save her tips and wages, which slowly accumulated until she had $ 3,000. Joe continued to paint houses in San Francisco, but he grew tired of the fine layer of flour covering everything in the house. Sixty-eight pounds of butter filled the refrigerator. Cases of yeast were stacked everywhere. Sacks of flour rested in mounds. "You have to get this out of the house," Joe advised. They began looking for a place to move and found an 850-square-foot building in Capitola at the corner of Bay and Capitola Avenue, the present location of Gayle's Bakery. Her father was in the restaurant equipment business, and when she came to him with the idea of opening a bakery, he tried to talk her out of it. He had seen too many restaurants go out of business and lose their homes, life savings, and investors' money. Gayle persisted and finally, he gave in, agreeing to match her $3000. Her sister knew a banker who would lend them another $3000. They accumulated $9000, which wasn't enough to open a bakery. Gayle went to the loan officer at Wells Fargo, who had loaned her the money for her Volkswagen, and he agreed to match what she had raised. She asked him to round it off to $10,000, and he agreed.

But she wasn't quite ready yet. "You have to have warm bread if you're going to run a bakery," her father insisted. They both looked at Joe, who could do anything. Bread dough looked like the spackle he used to fill cracks in a paint job, Joe reasoned, so, on that slim comparison, Joe began baking. Gayle gave him a 30-quart floor mixer, a 100-pound sack of flour, salt, yeast, and water, and Joe made baguettes. Gretchen Friedwald, a longtime friend and roommate who recently passed away, agreed to be the salesperson. Kelly Porter, who later opened Kelly's Bakery in Aptos, came to work the next week, and they launched the business, opening their doors on Valentine's Day, 1978.

"We worked our butts off," said Gayle. "We came to work at 3 a.m., and Joe left to paint houses at 8. He'd come back at 5 p.m.; we'd close at 6, spend an hour cleaning up, and then go home and eat dinner. Then we'd get up the next day and start all over again."

The Bakery made money from the beginning. But a year-and-a-half later, they needed an infusion of new recipes and techniques. Where did one go to learn baking? From the masters, of course. So Gayle and Joe headed to Paris. They wandered the streets checking with bakery owners who could teach them how to make French pastries. They weren't having any luck when, weary from being rejected, they chanced upon a sign for The Federation of French Bakers. The president saw them right away. In broken French, they told him they came to Paris to study baking and asked if he could recommend anyone. He went to a 25-foot-long card index that contained information on the federation's 1200 members and pulled out a single card. "He had the perfect man for us to study with," Gayle said. HIS NAME HERE and his wife loved foreigners. We've been back to study with him three times. He was the inspiration for Joe's book, The Village Baker.

Gayle attributes the success of the bakery to her customers, who are well-educated world travelers. Many are wealthy and sophisticated but want to live outside the glitter and bustle of a large city. Every day, she overheard customers commenting that they traveled all over the world but preferred to live here.

In 2001, Gayle said, "Santa Cruz has changed drastically since I opened my business 23 years ago. It's become a big city with traffic congestion and big box stores. If I didn't have the business, I don't know if I'd stay; my family and many friends moved away."

Yet she found a significant positive in the close-knit community. The community was a mere two-and-a-half square miles with a population of 10,000, made up of different neighborhoods. When she attended professional meetings in the San Francisco Bay area, she found that other business owners weren't willing to contribute to their communities. None of their communities knew what they contributed, an experience very different from Gayle's. The bakery gave to many local charities and events, and they thanked Gayle daily, a fact she attributed to people feeling a stronger connection to local businesses. As an illustration, she pointed to the difficulty national chains experienced when locals reacted negatively to the intrusion of Boston Market, Crown Books, Sizzler Restaurant, and Red Lobster, all of which went out of business despite extensive advertising. New developments by Borders Books and Home Depot also met considerable resistance.

"Lots of chains have trouble in this community," she said. "I feel a strong symbiosis with the community from living in Capitola. I live a block from city hall and know the firemen, the policemen, and the city council members, and there's something wonderful about that."

Her involvement with and concern for the community led to Gayle's decision to run for the city council despite the sometimes tumultuous and fractious debates that often racked the council. She was concerned about traffic and congestion because Capitola "was a bubble in a changing sea of traffic," a shortcut for those seeking to avoid Highway One. Zoning studies were in drastic need of revision. Her vision of Capitola was to keep the look and feel it had back in the 30s, 40s, and 50s, but with an updated economy; yesterday's physical layout with a modern economy. She sought to protect and upgrade the 41st Avenue corridor, where businesses produced city tax revenues to support the police and fire departments, public works projects, and many non-profit and city programs.

"Capitola has some of the best city services in California because we have 41st Avenue, and I want to make sure the business district remains viable," Gayle said. "I'm not anti-business or anti-big business; there's a size and place for everything. I'd like to see more hotels in Capitola and more cultural activities. The more hotels, the greater the sales tax revenue."

Her entrance into the fray of city government was based on a belief that the city council was more amenable to change. Although civility was essential to her, Gayle said she was a scrapper and would shout back if people shouted at her. In reality, she hoped for less screaming and fewer city council fights because the majority on the council was ushering in a new era. Rather than condemning the city decisions, as those who spoke out against the Redtree Properties development project for, or having an abrasive style, Gayle hoped to change the approach.

"We needed to move on to positive things, like the slow speed at which government moved, which is shocking when you're involved," Gayle said. She wanted to bring business skills to the process. "Why not run government like a business? Many say we can't continue doing business at a snail's pace. People must know they can effect change; we need another way of doing business in town hall politics."

The Barn in Scotts Valley, 1960

FINDING ONE'S MEDIUM: CLAIRE BRAZ VALENTINE ON BECOMING A PLAYWRIGHT
by Don Monkerud

An internationally known poet and playwright with many awards, Claire's play Women Behind the Walls, about incarcerated women, is a regular in theater classes. Her plays opened in Santa Cruz before going to Off Broadway in New York and overseas. Sponsored by the William James Association, which promotes work service in community service, education, and the environment, she was awarded their first Lifetime Achievement Award for 30 years of working with inmates in the California prison system. In 2018, she lost all her manuscripts and her home in the Paradise, California wildfire. Luckily, she escaped with her son, sister, and dog.

When Claire Braz Valentine received a call from theater director Michael Griggs asking her to help work out the problems with an ensemble group of actors in downtown Santa Cruz, she thought there must be some mistake.

"Sorry you have me mixed up with someone else," she told him. "I'm Claire Braz Valentine, the poet."

He knew who she was, and they talked on the phone while she busily prepared her sons' school lunches for the next day. Michael explained that he was asking six playwrights to come down for interviews to help with the play. Claire didn't mention that she didn't know what an ensemble or improv was, but she had promised herself long before not to turn down opportunities. She could only come down after five because she had a full-time job. That was fine with Michael, and they agreed on a date.

When Claire arrived at the theater, she found five male

playwrights who looked like she imagined playwrights should look: distinguished. One even smoked a pipe and had elbow patches on his jacket. The actors appeared mysterious, and the whole scene struck Claire as exotic. But she wondered what she could do to help them with their play. The actors performed a scene, and each playwright commented. When it came her turn, Claire asked each actor what they wanted to see onstage. What motivated their characters? What did their characters want?

"It turned out to be one of the most interesting evenings I've ever spent," contends Claire. "Because I was a fiction writer and worked with character, I thought I could give them insights into their characters. I could make some comments, which was a nice way to bow out gracefully. The cast left the room for ten minutes, and when they came back, they said, 'Congratulations, you're our new playwright.' I don't know what hit me first: joy or panic. Both emotions of joy and panic drive a playwright because playwriting is the most dangerous of all the writing arts. At any minute, all hell can break loose on stage."

Although Claire had written poetry for years and published articles in local papers such as the Good Times, The Phoenix, the Express, the Independent, and Taste, as well as national papers like SF Chronicle, LA Times, and SJ Mercury, she had never written a play. Terror struck on opening night, and she feared the play would be so bad that she couldn't show her face in town. A complex story with references to Mt. Shasta and filled with magic, rain and thunder, and trap doors, the play ushered people on and off stage in a flurry of movement and lighting quick changes. Although Claire admits she didn't understand what the play was about, it became a hit when critics discovered lofty ideas hidden in the plot. Each critic provided their own interpretation; several called the play brilliant, and Claire was on her way to a new career she'd never even dreamed of.

"I loved the actors, the stage managers, the dressers, the costumes, the lighting designers, the sound designers, and everything about the theater," Claire explains. "I wanted to do more plays."

She asked Michael Griggs to give her advice as she wrote her play, and he consented, which resulted in This One Thing I Do, a play about the 50-year struggle of Susan B. Anthony and Elizabeth Cady Stanton to win the women's right to vote. Although Claire had read poetry before plays at the Bear Republic Theater, now it was her play appearing on stage. This One Thing I Do opened on July 22, 1982, and after the play closed, Claire decided to start at the top and work her way down the list of publishers until she found someone to publish the play. She sent it to Samuel French, the largest publisher of plays in the world. After almost a year, a letter arrived containing what Claire describes as the finest sentence in the English language, "Congratulations, we're going to publish your play." The letter changed her life; she suddenly became "Claire Braz Valentine, the playwright," and decided to devote her life to playwriting.

Writing wasn't new to Claire; she'd been writing her whole life. Born into a working-class family in San Francisco, with an older brother and two younger sisters, Claire grew up in a one-bedroom Victorian flat at 17th and Vermont in a neighborhood that hasn't changed since her earliest memories. Her father was a Portuguese longshoreman who won respect as a left-wing militant and raised his family to believe that the worst violation in the world was to cross a picket line. Claire remembers her father spending half his time on strike while she was growing up, and he would disappear for days at a time, leaving the family without money to buy food. When he was home, his violent temper ruled the house, leading Claire to describe her childhood as "treacherous." Her mother was an orphan whose mother died of TB after immigrating from Ireland, and her grandfather abandoned the family. In 1890 her grandmother and her three sisters became indentured servants, sailed to America, and came through Ellis Island.

Claire attended elementary school at the Immaculate Conception Academy, a Catholic school at 24th and Guerrero. In elementary school, Claire wrote poetry and read voraciously, often coming home from the library with armloads of books. Shy around boys, she didn't mix well, and switched to a public junior high school, and withdrew into a world of books. Claire was overjoyed when her mother relented and let her return to Catholic school.

"I walked into class to find 30 girls and felt like I'd come home," Claire recalls. "Within a year, I was in every club. I became the journalism editor, the scientific newsletter editor, the class clown, and the head of the drama club. I loved it and didn't have to worry about my shyness because, you see, I wasn't shy around girls. I learned to bond with girls and to trust myself and my art. I learned the joy of writing, and the nuns convinced me my mind was powerful. Many people like to put down Catholic School, but I have no negative feelings towards the nuns or my education; they did nothing but good for me."

"The same girl who wanted to go to a girl's school ended up working the majority of her time in a room full of male felons," she said. "I learned so much from them. I was a mother teaching other mother's sons, and my students gave me so much joy, respect, and trust."

Claire wrote her first play in high school when the drama club was asked to present a Shakespeare play. The girls didn't look forward to gluing beards on their faces to play men's roles, nor twisting their tongues around the Old English pronunciation. The girls hated the play and told Claire to tell Sister Mary Edward they did not want to do it. Sister Mary Edward would have to find a different play for them. The sister refused. If the girls wanted another play, Claire would have to write it for them. Claire protested that she couldn't do it, but the sister insisted. Despite her youth, Claire wrote and performed in her first play at age 16.

Claire had a rich social life in what many describe as a restrictive Catholic School. Because every Catholic Girl's school is paired with a Catholic Boy's school, students attend each other's social events, such as dances and football games. That event occurred every weekend, and San Francisco presented Claire and her friends with the whole city as a playground. One friend's father owned an ice cream store, and the girls would recklessly race the father's pickup truck up and down the steep hills, winding up at the ice cream fountain at midnight, where they would eat ice cream and play the jukebox until all hours of the morning. Their escapades recall the innocence of youth before drugs and birth control pills were available. Back then, if a girl became pregnant, she married or went to a home for unwed mothers. Such consequences kept Claire on a straight and narrow path compared to the rebelliousness of later generations.

A bright student, she can't remember a time when she wasn't writing during elementary and high school. Claire wanted to go to college, but her father absolutely refused to assist her. A violent scene with her father drove the point home, and she turned to her high school boyfriend for solace. He came from a nice family, and they married a year after high school.

"I was going to be Betty Crocker and make the type of

home that I had always wanted to grow up in," Claire said. "I gave it a good run. I had three sons, who are the mainstays of my life. They are, for me, my finest accomplishment, and it still feels strange—they are now 36, 38, and 40—not to have them living with me. My life was so intense with my boys and their friends who hung out at our house. It wasn't uncommon to wake up in the morning and find their friends in sleeping bags on my living room floor. I still see many of them; they're still part of the family. It's very difficult to let go of that period of my life."

After getting married, Claire helped put her husband through school, and once he received his engineering degree, they moved to Sunnyvale, where he opened his own business. Between raising her boys, Claire continued writing stories, chiefly for them, and published them in boy's magazines. She joined a writing group at the Stanford Free University, taught by Ed McClannan, an associate of Ken Kesey's, and discovered a whole new world. The first night she attended a class, she found an unfamiliar scene: a bathtub lined with foam rubber filled one room and a house full of young hippies. She felt like little Mrs. Homemaker in her housedress, girdle, nylons, and high heels. In contrast to her tight, convoluted, and cryptic poems, the other participants wrote what Claire describes as "raw, open, emotional, narrative poetry, powerful stuff that I'd never even dreamed about." Claire soon abandoned the nylons, girdles, and bra and her poetry became less inhibited.

Because her husband spent so much time at his new business, Claire spent most of her time alone. She began to feel like she was Betty Crocker abandoned without Mr. Crocker. Social changes contributed to her feelings, for this was a time of social ferment; Vietnam War protests wracked the country, and the women's movement was spreading. She began to feel trapped as a housewife and feared spending the rest of her life living in the suburbs, hosting cocktail parties for her husband and his business cronies. Claire recalls meeting an impressive woman artist, and when Claire told her that she felt like a square peg trying to bash herself into a round hole, the woman told her to take pride in herself; there were enough round pegs already and too few square pegs.

"I felt an enormous gaping horrible lack and emptiness in my life," Claire recalls. "After 13 years of marriage, I realized that my husband and I were no longer good for each other. I'd long since stopped loving him, although he was a fine man. He raised not only our children but me, too, but I'd grown into a very different person than the one he married. I wanted a different life."

With the divorce, her life changed radically; she had to get a job and became the primary support for her three sons. Not to be stymied, she continued to freelance articles to magazines and to write poetry and humor. Despite focusing on her sons and writing, her life expanded. She joined psychodrama and encounter groups, attended anti-war marches, and began inviting interesting people over for dinner. She removed everything from her house's walls and redecorated it with seashells, rocks, and candles. She gave a party and wound up standing on the couch in the living room reading from Richard Brautigan. She published poetry, and her picture appeared on the front page of the Sunday Pictorial Living section in the San Francisco Chronicle, identifying her as a poet and short story writer.

"It's important to remember that I never had training to be a writer," Claire cautions. "I wasn't inhibited about my field, and I didn't know that people identified as poets, journalists, or short story writers. I thought I'd just be a writer."

Although she tried to work part-time and attend college, there were no grants for young mothers, and she had to return to work full-time. She purchased a house in San Jose from her share of the divorce proceeds and made a commercial advertising Cascade dishwashing soap for national TV, for which she received $9,000, a considerable sum at the time and enough to help make ends meet. She fell in love with a man who was ten years younger, and after 18 months, they decided to live together.

"All hell broke loose," Claire explains. "My father refused to see me, my ex-husband took me to court to take the kids away, and one of my sisters stopped talking to me. We decided to get married and move to Memphis, Tennessee."

Claire describes herself as "a one-woman man" and remained monogamous, despite an agreement with her husband that they would get married for the world, but wouldn't "feel married." She felt freer in spirit and had what she describes as a short, wondrous adventure. In Memphis, Claire discovered that her Betty Crocker days were indeed over; she didn't fit in with the Southern belles. She became a department manager at the University of Tennessee, joined a women's consciousness-raising group, and became active in the National Organization for Women. But she missed California.

"I longed for the ocean," she recounts. "One day, I parked on the banks of the Mississippi and begged the river to fill the hollow aching in my soul for the seashore. The river couldn't do it. I decided I never wanted to live outside California again; I never wanted to be away from the coast for the rest of my life."

Claire moved to Boulder Creek, where she lived for eight years because she knew there were many writers in the area. She took a job at the university, eventually becoming an office manager for the Board of Studies and Literature, and immediately made contact with other women writers.

She bought a house in the early 1970s, where she began her playwriting career. The house became a nesting place where she could raise her sons, write, and put a log on the fire in the wintertime. She felt at home. A few years later, she came to the breakfast table on Christmas morning and told her sons they wouldn't be in the house the following Christmas. She couldn't explain why, but despite her sons' protest—one of them had to commute to San Lorenzo High to graduate—they moved. The following winter, a tree crushed the house, destroying her son's bedrooms but sparing the new owners sleeping in the master bedroom. Feeling fortunate that her sons' lives were spared, she settled into her house on the West Side of Santa Cruz and continued to work at UCSC.

After her initial success in playwriting, Claire stopped writing as much poetry as she had formerly done and, for an extended period, devoted herself to writing plays and working. Her years of writing produced Blue Skies Forever, a story of Amelia Earhart that went straight to New York City after playing in Santa Cruz. In researching the play, she interviewed people who knew George Putnam, Amelia Earhart's manager, only to discover that he wasn't likable. Because her plays focus on women, she wrestled with how to write the role for Putnam and solved the dilemma by collaborating with her male friends. "Does this sound like a man?" she would ask. In the long run, she decided that her men sounded like men because she got help unwittingly from the actors. Because men played men's roles, they had the same motivation as her male characters and brought their interpretation to the roles.

Claire considers her next play, When Will I Dance, a play about Frida Kahlo, her favorite because it doesn't follow the typical play structure. The play ran for a year in Helsinki and played in other major cities worldwide. She considers When Will I Dance her masterpiece.

"One review called Frida a poetic masterpiece because it's like a long prose poem," she says. "It's very unusual because it uses theater in a new way. There are two people in the play, and they are both Frida Kahlo. I'm not interested in writing standard storytelling drama. I just don't have the desire. I like to bend time and space and create magic on the stage. Not magic in a hokey sense, but in a way that respects the audience and challenges me to be better than I can be by writing up to them. Of course, it helps only to tackle projects I'm 100 percent behind."

That challenge is brought home when a play contains a weak line. A strong poem can carry a few weak poems in a book of poetry, but that doesn't happen in a play performed before a live audience. A weak line can begin to lose the audience, and if they start thinking about something else, they're gone. That's why Claire views playwriting as "the most dangerous art."

During those years of writing, working, and raising her sons, when she wrote Blue Skies Forever and When Will I Dance, her work became the background of her family life. Two incidents brought this home to her. One night, while she completed a short story, one of her son's friends picked up the manuscript and found her name on it.

"You wrote this?" he wondered. "I didn't know you were a writer."

"What did you think I was doing sitting here at the typewriter every night?" she asked.

"Typing," he responded.

Another time, her son had trouble sleeping, and she asked if a warm glass of milk would help. He said no, it wouldn't, but if she could type for half an hour, he could go to sleep.

Despite her success at playwriting, her plays didn't bring

financial independence. Claire continued working at UCSC, although when they lowered the retirement age to 50, she decided to fulfill her life's dream and devote herself to writing. She would support herself with her small retirement package by teaching in the Spectra Program in public schools and giving her workshops.

"I retired from the university because I didn't have to support my kids anymore," she says. "It was just me, and if I went belly up, I'd be the only one floating in the bowl. I felt like a fish; I would place myself next to the edge of the water and wait for the tide to come in, and when it did, I'd jump in. The tide came in, I jumped, and I've been swimming ever since."

The first year after quitting her full-time job presented a real challenge. Finding it difficult to organize her various projects, Claire got five different briefcases. She wouldn't have to empty the work and keep track of it by keeping all the work pertaining to one project in each briefcase. Slowly, she got a handle on her new career. The Spectra project included teaching elementary and high school classes, and after judging writing contests in the California State Prisons, the men's prison at Soledad prison asked her to teach. Several years later, she began teaching at Chowchilla State Prison, a women's prison, where she wrote and produced the play Women Behind the Walls with the inmates. Since then, she has conducted workshops in most of the state prisons, and when Salinas Valley State Prison, a new maximum security facility, couldn't find a teacher, she took the job where she taught two classes a week.

"I love working in the prisons," she said. "I like working with inmates who are making art against all odds. I became a writer against all odds; with no training, no support, no mentors, and out of desperation, I broke into the field on my own. I can walk into the prison and say, 'If I can do it, you can do it. I'll give you something I never had. I'll show you step-by-step how to do it.' I can bring blessings to their lives. We make a holy place to write together out of the chaos and hell of prison. It brings peace to their lives. That's what it takes to succeed. People in touch with the artist in themselves are less likely to return to prison. It's an enormous job. Some of the men I work with will never get out of prison, but writing helps them find solace and gives them a way to cope with the dreary existence of prison."

In addition to working with adult prisoners, Claire has taught at Redwood Treatment Center, a juvenile hall facility and residential drug treatment center for teens who commit felonies. Her work there produced a play, Listen to Our Voices, which toured the alternative high schools in Santa Cruz County. Claire feels she can relate to the teenagers due to her own experiences growing up when she wore hand-me-downs and often went hungry. She finds that many teenagers come from homes like the one she grew up in, except she didn't have the drugs that kids have now. If she had, she might very well have been in the same situation, except the nuns and her mother helped keep her together, and she can provide a role for troubled teenagers.

Claire found the support, feedback, and encouragement from the community of women writers in Santa Cruz made her realize she was no longer a square peg trying to fit into a round hole. She feels fortunate that she could grow and fulfill her dream of becoming a writer, a goal she pursues even in retirement. In addition to her teaching, she worked on a new play, Hope, about her grandmother and other immigrants coming through Ellis Island on their way to a new life in America. Despite her love for puttering around the house, playing with her dog, Barkley, and her addiction to rewriting—

she calls herself "a rewriting junkie"—Claire organizes her days around writing.

"The thought of not working terrifies me," Claire said. "I can't imagine it. Finally, I have enough time to write—the one thing I really want to do. Some days, I wake up with a pencil in my hand and papers strewn around me on the bed. At night, I fall asleep in the middle of writing a sentence."

"Mary Holmes, gifted artist. told me once that the reason she didn't exhibit her later work was that she painted 'for the grace of God.' Since the fire, I write for the grace of God."

Three Psychic Physicists: Nick Herbert, Ralph Abraham, Bruce Damer

LAST LUNCH WITH RALPH
By Bruce Damer

This past month we lost a mathematical giant and surfer of conscious states at the very edge of chaos: Ralph Abraham. Along with Rupert Sheldrake and Terence McKenna he was third member of the Trialogues, epic conversations recorded in the 80s and 90s which mesmerized and challenged a new generation of seekers (including me). I have a lot to thank Ralph for. Back in 1998 he drove Terence and his son Finn (just turned twenty) up here to Ancient Oaks. This act set off a pinball run of events in my life lasting until today.

After Terence's passing, Ralph and I got to know each other much better. He drove up here again a decade later to deliver a box of cassette tapes of the whole Trialogue series. Instead of being lost to analogue history, these digitized recordings helped power up the Psychedelic Salon Podcast. We started to meet periodically for lunch in Santa Cruz talking metaphysics, mathematics, psychedelics and abiogenetics. I also joined his Hip Santa Cruz project, sitting in story circles 2-3 times per year to capture the remarkable oral history of aging but very lucid counterculture figures and their transformative effect on society. Ralph also supported my DigiBarn Computer Museum by donating numerous artifacts including his network of early NeXT Computers which were used to visualize math (including those famous strange attractors).

His story of how psychedelics (particularly LSD) powered insights for his mathematics from the 1960s powered my own interest in the topic. I cited Ralph's 2008 essay Mathematics and the Psychedelic Revolution in my coming-out-of-the-psychedelic-scientist-closet article It's High Time for Science. His definitive telling of the story of psychedelic evolution of tech and math helped charge up the case for the creation of the Center for MINDS itself:

"There is no doubt that the psychedelic evolution in the 1960s had a profound effect on the history of computers and computer graphics, and of mathematics, especially the birth of postmodern maths such as chaos theory and fractal geometry. This I witnessed personally. The effect on my own history, viewed now in four decades of retrospect, was a catastrophic shift from abstract pure math to a more experimental and applied study of vibrations and forms, which continues to this day." - Ralph Abraham

At our last lunch back in March, 2024, 87 year-old Nick Herbert, one of our prized residents here at Ancient Oaks, joined me to meet with 87 year-old Ralph. They both moved to the Santa Cruz Mountains in the late 60s and crossed paths many times socially. It was delightful to witness two true wizards in (sometimes hilarious) discourse!

Ralph's legacy goes on, from his many books and articles, pioneering work in dynamical systems theory and math visualization, and aiding society through his work guiding young people to enter exciting creative lives at the Ross School, and his visionary quest for an Akashic physics with Kolkata mathematician Sisir Roy.

My final thoughts and feelings go out to his lovely wife and partner of many decades, "Rainbow" Ray Gwyn Smith.

Note

Nick Herbert is the author of Quantum Reality, Anchor Books, 1987.

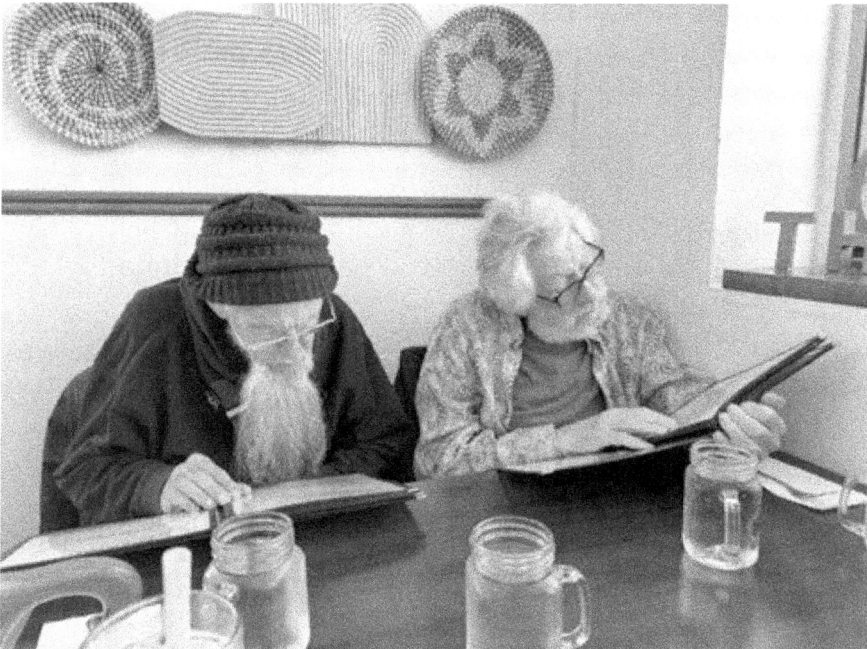

Nick Herbert and Ralph Abraham

FROM MATH TO MUSHROOMS, INTELLECTUAL EXPLORER RALPH ABRAHAM WAS ALWAYS LOOKING FOR THE BIG PICTURE

By Wallace Baine
Lookout Santa Cruz

In the final months of Ralph Abraham's life, Kathleen Harrison, a close family friend going back decades, would often visit him at his Bonny Doon home. And, in the quiet moments, when he was dozing, Harrison would find herself perusing her friend's heaving bookshelves. What struck her was not only that there were always a handful of newer non-fiction titles that she had never noticed before, but the obvious rigor at which all these books had been read.

"Every single one of them — and I'm not exaggerating — every single book had dozens of little sticky notes, pink and yellow, marking every quote that mattered to him," she said. "I would always look for an interesting title or an interesting topic, and I'd wonder if that [author] realized that Ralph Abraham read their book so carefully that it had 24, 25 different sticky notes in it."

The other thing to note about Abraham's books was the astonishing range of interests, a range that many might intellectually aspire to, but few in fact achieve. His interests included everything from engineering and mathematics (his chosen field), to European Enlightenment philosophy, to the science of psychedelics, to Hindu scholarship, to Jewish mysticism.

"I was surprised to discover," said Harrison, "an entire section on Celtic mythology, which I know something about. Yet, we never got around to talking about it."

Abraham died on Sept. 19 at the age of 88, quieting not only one of the most formidable minds in Santa Cruz County, but perhaps even in American academia. He is best known for his groundbreaking work in pure mathematics, namely in the fields of Chaos Theory and Field Dynamical Systems.

At the same time, he is a seminal figure in the 1960s counterculture, particularly as it applies to the pursuit of self-enlightenment through psychedelics and Eastern mysticism (and, at least in Abraham's case, math). For years, he has been engaged in an ongoing writing project, titled "Hip Santa Cruz," in which he has documented through first-hand witnesses the "miracle," as he called it, of the '60s counterculture through the prism of Santa Cruz. Yet, into his 80s, Abraham was also a man of the modern world, performing as an electronica musician and writing on such contemporary obsessions as A.I.

He is the author of more than a dozen books, most notably a series of "trialogues" with fellow counterculture intellectual icons biologist Rupert Sheldrake and ethnobotanist Terence McKenna called "Chaos, Creativity and Cosmic Consciousness."

In my interviews and encounters with Abraham over the years, he was always ready to undermine the assumption that math was his "day job" that allowed him to follow his real passion, the quest for transcendence. In fact, mathematics was part of — perhaps even the most central and relevant part of — the effort to better understand the underlying nature of existence. Math was the skeleton key, in his view, of unlocking the "structures of consciousness."

And that mind was still spinning at the end. His wife, Ray Gwyn Smith, said that Abraham was even planning to write another book, on a very pertinent subject in 2024, before time ran out on him.

"What he was working on before he got really ill," she said, "was about the madness of crowds and how the Internet has been influencing politics."

The Coming of Abraham

The story of how Ralph Abraham ended up in Santa Cruz is full of impulsive acts and serendipity.

The defining characteristic of his early life in the 1940s was a diagnosis of tuberculosis while he was still a teen. A last-minute development of an antibiotic saved his life, but the disease put him in bed for two years at a time when others his age were in the throes of high school. In his last weeks, Abraham mentioned to his friend Kathleen Harrison that "I wouldn't have been the person I am if I had not spent those years as an adolescent, not sure if I were going to live or die." He called the period "the longest meditation of my life."

As a young scholar, he followed his curiosity from electrical engineering to physics to pure mathematics, earning his Ph.D. at the age of 23 from the University of Michigan, and then landing teaching jobs at UC Berkeley, Columbia and Princeton.

UC Santa Cruz was established in 1965, based on a kind of Oxford-style model of alternative education. Abraham was exactly the kind of young thinker the new university was looking for. He was recruited to join the UCSC faculty in 1968, and Abraham said, he didn't take the job or the university too seriously at the time. He used the job offer as an excuse for a trip to California to see friends. He was intent on returning to Princeton when one of those friends, author Jim Houston, suggested his stop by a nightclub in Scotts Valley called The Barn.

"I saw the musicians playing inside large metal sculptures, psychedelic paintings on the wall and 300 naked people stoned on LSD dancing to the music," he said. "I was in heaven."

Later, as a university professor, he bought an enormous, 24-room Victorian mansion on California Street, near Santa Cruz High School. It was there that Abraham presided over a hippie-style bacchanal of students and teachers, musicians and mystics, wanderers and curiosity-seekers.

"I never lived in such an intense, hippie-crash-pad, creative-chaos kind of scene like that ever again," said Harrison.

"It was the hub of hip Santa Cruz," said Smith. "The Merry Pranksters, and Ram Dass, and just everybody you could think of would wind up at that house."

Abraham had first tried LSD in 1967 while at Princeton, and by the time he arrived in Santa Cruz, he was in full embrace of the radical subculture of the time. At a rally, he wore an Abbie Hoffman-style American flag shirt and was photographed with his friend and colleague Paul Lee. That photo ran on the front pages of many newspapers across the country. Having negotiated tenure as part of his UCSC job, Abraham was protected. Lee was not, and was later forced out.

The Really Big Picture

Of Abraham's use of LSD and other psychedelics, his friend Harrison said, "They were very helpful to him in allowing him to get to a perspective where he could see the Really Big Picture, from the minutiae to the cosmos. And to find ways of describing it more mathematically than in any other way."

He would also often take sabbaticals and travel to

India, to meditate and study with yogi masters (later, he also embraced India music, playing the tabla). He was developing an avid interest in the varieties of psychedelic experiences and psychedelic substances. He sought out many of the great thinkers and philosophers and mystics of the era. He was criticial in the development of Chaos Theory in mathematics and contributed greatly to its understanding.

Those close to him say that, behind much of Abraham's relentless curiosity about the big themes of existence was a desire to become the best person he could be.

"Ralph had such a gentle, soft sense of humor," said Harrison, "and there was so little judgment about other people. For a person with a pretty good intuitive discernment about what a good person is, he didn't have any mean humor in him. And I was always moved by that. How does he stay so tender-hearted and still engage with so many different people."

"I got a chance to visit him about a week before he died," said longtime friend and former student Peter Broadwell. "And he said [about dying], 'There's a chance I'm going to find a whole bunch of other things to explore.' He was always such an inquisitive mind. He was frustrated his body was failing him. But his mind was exploring still."

In his later years, said wife Ray Gwyn Smith, he had achieved a level of fame for his groundbreaking works in mathematics, and some in the rarefied field of math spoke his name in reverence. But Abraham himself was rarely impressed by such things.

"He was just completely unaffected by his high profile," she said. "He was just such a gentle, kind, loving person, with so much integrity. He had this very limitless kind of understanding of the world, and that was what was so exciting about him."

Ralph and Ray at home

Ralph and Ray Abraham at Tomales Bay, CA

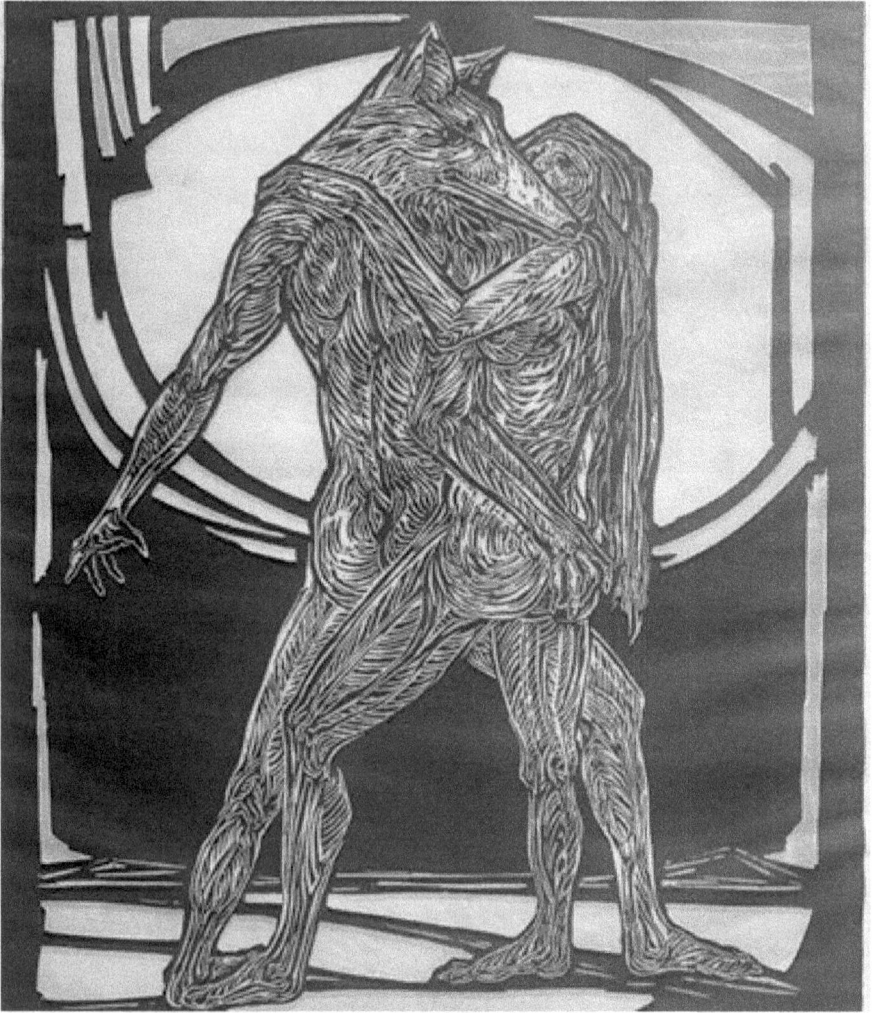

Coyote and his Woman, Daniel O. Stolpe

www.ingramcontent.com/pod-product-compliance
Lightning Source LLC
Chambersburg PA
CBHW052344090426
42739CB00011B/2304